CW01083667

THE *UNPLUGGED*

SUMMER

AN ENGLISHMAN'S PERSPECTIVE OF LIFE AT AN AMERICAN SUMMER CAMP

GEORGE HORNER

Copyright © 2019 by George Horner. All Rights Reserved.

All rights reserved. No part of this book may be reproduced in any form or by any electronic or mechanical means including information storage and retrieval systems, without permission in writing from the author. The only exception is by a reviewer, who may quote short excerpts in a review.

ISBN 978-1-7287-5764-3

Cover designed by Ansh Deb

The right of George Horner to be identified as the author of this work has been asserted by him in accordance with the Copyright, Designs and Patents Act 1988.

To my family—love you all.

And to the cups of tea and coffee—my companions through the many long days of writing, as well as the hangovers.

CONTENTS

The following is based on real events, with settings and conversations recreated from my memories of them. To maintain confidentiality, I have altered information, appearances and changed all the names (apart from my brothers) of those I've encountered in this memoir.

INTRODUCTION:
NEW BEGINNINGS

It's the beginning of June 2015, and my current employment is nearly at an end. Soon, I'll be leaving my job in England as a caregiver and teaching assistant at a residential school for children with physical and learning disabilities. I have just two more weeks of work to go, and then I'll be entering a place of uncertainty—but it's a place that I'm willing to engage with.

I'm determined to involve myself in a potentially memorable summer with new people from all different backgrounds. After all, a life can be destroyed in an instant, whether by a tragic car accident or the doctor sitting you down and breaking the bad news. So why shouldn't I take this opportunity?

Plus, I'm 23 years old. I'm not getting any younger, and this is the perfect time in my life to start traveling. No tie-backs or big commitments—just me to worry about. My only *personal* responsibilities will be letting my family and close friends know that I'm safe and enjoying myself.

Lately, at the dinner table, my dad has repeatedly asked:

"Not long 'til you go now, George. Are you looking forward to it?"

Of course, I always answer "Yes."

My family is right to be interested, although I sense their apprehension. I too am feeling anxious, but by the same token, I want a change of scenery and new beginnings with fresh faces. Hopefully, I'll find all of this in America.

Throughout my summers as a student, I've stayed nearby to the town I live in, doing the occasional summer work here and there. I've been a cleaner, a food runner in a restaurant, and a manual laborer in a warehouse. All of these jobs were temporary, just so I could have cash in my pocket to enjoy the summer with my friends.

Back when my brothers and I were little, we spent summer weeks away with our parents on Hayling Island, not far from where we live in Hampshire. We stayed in a caravan that was owned by my grandparents, situated on a bumpy, gritty road. The road was home to many other caravans, but it was still a picturesque environment.

On Hayling Island, we relished in our adventures on the beach and in the surrounding marsh lakes, where we would go crabbing. We hiked to the lakes with our plastic buckets and spades, and our bait of ham attached to reels, which delved into the muddy waters until crabs were hooked. We lifted them into our yellow buckets, proud of our bounty. The helpless crabs were then poured out to return to their homes on the lakes.

We also kept ourselves entertained in the amusement parks, particularly with the 2-pence and 10-pence slot machines. Not far from there, we'd traditionally spend a day at the Funfair, which was about a mile walk down from the beach. And on those sunny days, during a coastal walk, we'd be taking in the views with our favorite ice cream slowly melting.

A couple of times during my childhood, we embarked on summer holidays at Butlins—a family holiday park. This was seemingly popular at the time when holidays abroad were less commercialized. Around this time, my brothers' and my interest in English football began, and we kicked around a soft, inflatable football, amidst the mini-Astroturf pitches, whenever we could. We always played while wearing our favorite football shirts. I vividly remember myself at the age of six, wearing a green Liverpool goalie shirt. My brother Chris, aged 10 at the time, wore a red Manchester United shirt. My oldest brother Tom, aged 12, wore a white shirt representing Tottenham Hotspur football club, aka the Spurs. A year or so later, we watched our first live football match as a family at the White Hart Lane Stadium. There, we all fell in love with the same club, and eventually, we all followed the Spurs.

Regardless of all the rows and arguments we've had over the years, football has played a crucial part in maintaining the strong bond I have with my brothers. On occasions, we boys still wear our latest Spurs shirts while cheering our team on the TV at our house or a local pub in town. Sometimes, we're lucky enough to watch them at the stadium. We condemn the opposition's team and praise our own. This becomes even more evident when our rival team—the Arsenal—arrives on the field.

Back to the topic of summer holidays— there were week- or fortnight-long stays at villages in Cornwall, Weymouth, and Bournemouth during my childhood and adolescence. We never traveled far as a family on holidays. Instead, we stayed close to home and hoped that warm weather and sunshine would appear. This was wishful thinking, considering that England is renowned for unpredictable weather.

Apart from vacations abroad with school and college groups, I haven't explored outside of the UK with my family. There was, however, one summer in 2001 when we traveled over to Alicante in Spain to show off our white *milk-bottle* bodies in the high heat. We stayed in a villa with a swimming pool. This was another property owned by my grandparents and they welcomed us there as the hosts.

During a couple of other summers, we visited Mum's side of the family, our distant relatives who live in southern Ireland. On these occasions, Dad drove countless miles to a ferry in Wales that got us over to the Irish coastline. He then drove to our destination, which was County Wicklow, south of Dublin. It was especially nice for Mum to return to the many acres of green countryside and catch up with her relatives, as well as visiting her mum's grave. Dad then had the long journey home to look forward to, of course.

But all these summer breaks that I've experienced only lasted a day or a couple of weeks at most—and although I'll always treasure these family holidays, I now want a worthwhile experience that will last for months, and that will be unforgettable.

1

THE FIRST STEP

Let me take you back to September 2014, when I took the plunge and applied to a recruitment agency called Wild Packs, which transfers young people to summer camp placements scattered across the Northeast region of America. The Wild Packs website has vibrant colors and persuasive language that intrigued me:

Around 10 million campers and goodness knows how many staff have the most amazing summers of their lives—become a counselor today!

The many slogans and positive testimonials on the website about summer camp life won me over, and I became desperate to be a part of it. This leads me to the first step of my journey to America—I have to fill out an application provided by Wild Packs. It requires me to write passages about my previous experiences in education and employment. It also requires me to write about the sports I'm best at. I've been very sporty since a young age, particularly in track and field events in the athletics season at school, and of course my beloved football, or what the Americans like to call *soccer!*

I also indicate to the agency that I'm a great person to supervise and look after the welfare of children and encouraging them to relish in all types of sports and leisure activities. This is evident in my present job, where I'm supporting the daily living and education of children with various disabilities. All of this information will show the agency what assets I have, which determines how valuable of a member I'd be at camp.

Since I'm required to provide my mobile number and email address to the agency as contact details, communication between us will now become a regular thing. I then receive a phone call.

"Hi George, it's Heather here from Wild Packs, just letting you know that your application is looking good and we have you linked to a camp already. You should be expecting an email very soon from them to arrange an interview with you!"

"Thank you, Heather. I'm glad you've received my application, and I'll look forward to hearing about the next steps I need to take."

After the phone conversation, I go onto my Outlook email account and there's an email from Mike, the staffing coordinator of the summer camp, stating that his camp has me on review with Wild Packs. Mike writes that he's interested in speaking with me about a position this summer. My ideal position is a "general counselor."

He asks me if I'm available for a Skype interview. We eventually agree on a time to talk. It will be on a Thursday, during the school's October half-term.

2

THE INTERVIEW

Let's fast-forward to an hour before the interview is to start—I'm not concerned about looking smart for it. Instead, I'm concerned about saying the right things to the questions. It's about meeting Mike's expectations. I've visited a few websites to gather sufficient information about what the most common questions are from a summer camp employer, and what answers give the best impression that I'll be a great summer camp counselor.

I'm not a huge fan of Skype. I don't like the idea of looking at the other person during conversation when we're separated by hundreds or thousands of miles. This is probably because I've become accustomed to talks on the telephone. I'm often awestruck at the way we can talk to each other with the simple touch of a few buttons. This all started from the world-changing invention of the telephone that allows us to talk freely to anyone—at any time, any place, anywhere. It amazes me that phones were ever invented, let alone all the other interactive devices using artificial intelligence that we have nowadays. It's like we're all in this imaginary dimension and anything is possible. It makes me wonder what the future will bring. It's crazy when you think about this so deeply and start to question the meaning of life. Society seems to distract us from these deep thoughts with the implementation of mass media, commercialization, and an endless supply of inventions.

I shift away from these thoughts and sit in the lounge with just my laptop in front of me. After reviewing the possible questions that I hope will come up in the interview, it's time for my call.

The anticipated jingle from Skype begins. After waiting a few seconds, I press the video call icon, and there he is. There's silence for a moment as I stare at him on the screen.

"Hi, George; how's it going?"

"Hi, Mike; I'm okay, thanks. How're you?"

I'm feeling a little uneasy at first. I guess interviews aren't something you do often, and although this interview is intended to be less serious, compared to a typical face-to-face job interview, it's still something that I haven't encountered many times before. Mike's accent really puts it into perspective that I'm applying for a job in America.

"So, you put on the application that you enjoy sports, and particularly soccer. Tell me more about that, George."

I tell Mike that I started playing English football when I was six years old, following in the footsteps of my brothers, who also participated in the sport throughout childhood. I've played on the county and district level for teams, and I've been successful in receiving several trophies throughout my years of participation. A few of these awards were for my personal efforts at the clubs, and others were from winning leagues and cups with the teams. He then asks if I follow a football team, and I said I'm a Spurs fan.

"No way! I'm a big Tottenham fan!" Mike said with amazement.

We start talking about all the great players over the years, such as the Irish striker, Robbie Keane, and Gareth Bale, also known as *the Welsh wizard*. We then talk about the exciting football that former manager, Harry Redknapp, had brought to the club. Plus, it turns out that Mike lived in London throughout his teens, and that he bought a season ticket to watch the football team play frequently. Mike has put me at ease, and it feels as if I were speaking to a good mate of mine in a local pub.

Mike then gives me a few questions, which I've thankfully anticipated.

"So, after looking at our website, what made you want to join us?"

"Err...it seems like you have a happy atmosphere. You offer a lot of great sports facilities for the campers, and in addition to the hard work of the staff members, there seems to be a lot of fun and entertainment."

I thought this answer goes without saying for most summer camps. Mike then tells me about what this summer camp entails. He says that his camp is in the populous American state of Massachusetts. It's an all-boys camp dedicated to mainstream sports, and the activities are run by professional coaches.

American children go to summer camps for a break away from their challenging school lives, yet at this camp, they are also there to develop their skills in various sports. The philosophy of Mike's camp is centered on teamwork. This philosophy is useful in the sports played and to help the groups around the camp function together constructively.

"A lot of these boys play for academy teams back where they live, and want to become athletes, so it's important that you take each of their activities seriously," said Mike.

I feel a bit bemused because I expected summer camps to be a relaxed environment for children—an environment where the children can have fun participating in the sports they love. I expected a more *it's the participation that counts* philosophy, but, instead, the camp seems to have a regimented program. The camp also takes curfews seriously, which is appropriate in terms of promoting the professionalism that's expected from the staff and the safety that's required for the children. But the regulations do seem to be very strict.

"Obviously, we like our staff to have fun with each other, and you may want to take a trip to the local bar one evening when you're off shift. But when you come back before the curfew ends, we need to make sure you are in working order to look after your children in the cabin. So, we might ask you a few questions, and even check your eyes and test them under the light."

Mike then opens it up for me to ask some questions. I ask him a few questions to continue showing interest and to evoke a good impression.

"What's the ratio between counselors and campers in an activity group?"

It's typically three campers to one counselor.

To end the interview, Mike thanks me for talking to him, and says that he'll be getting in touch about organizing a second interview for me to engage with the camp's director. Although it comes as frustrating news to have the extra stress of a further interview, I suppose that it's all part of the selection process. They want to make sure that the people they recruit will last the eight or nine weeks of employment. They also want to make sure I'll have the patience and flexibility to supervise and look after the children, while enabling them to have fun. It's a big commitment.

3

MY PREFERENCES

The next couple of weeks involve messages from Mike and the summer camp director, whose name is Jared. I once again go back and forth scheduling the second Skype interview, this time with Jared. I'm at work, on two occasions, when they ask me to contact them, which causes me some annoyance. I prefer it when a plan is made in advance, though the daily schedule of a summer camp director appears to be too chaotic to make that happen.

Eventually, after discussing it over with my family, I decide that I don't want to be considered as an employee for this camp. This is fundamentally down to the seriousness of teaching sports to the children, and the disciplinary actions toward staff. I sensed an unrelaxed atmosphere. Maybe it's just me being too judgmental, but I now want to see what else is out there.

I email Mike and Jared, stating that I feel their camp isn't the right one for me. My main reason to them is that I'd like to work with children in a wider variety of leisure activities. Preferably, I want a less serious focus on sports and an inclusion of non-sport activities, such as arts and crafts. I was graded well at school in this subject and it provided great enjoyment to me as a student. I still take a liking to artistic creations, especially when viewing my brother's art exhibitions. Unlike me, Chris's passion for art still remains. Chris has a talent in modern art, particularly with creating fascinating sculptures out of undesirable materials. He fits his creative work around his job at the local supermarket.

A few weeks after my decision to reject Mike, I get another setback in reaching an agreement with a summer camp on my radar. This is from an all-boys overnight summer camp that's located five hours north of Chicago. They participate in an array of land and water sports. The activities on offer include water skiing, climbing, sailing, canoeing, archery, and riflery. The non-negotiation for this one came when the summer camp director stated in his email that he can *"easily see me* as guy who helps instruct some of our land sports, while also getting certified on our climbing tower." Assisting in the safety of the campers' participation and encouraging the fun aspect of land activities isn't problem.

On the other hand, I'll be unable to function if I'm in high, open surroundings, such as standing on the edge of a cliff. A feeling of vertigo runs through me if I'm in this situation. Therefore, I can't see myself acting professional enough to instruct and motivate children to climb tower when I would fear it myself.

The camp's director also stated that they need their international staff members to be lifeguard certified. Swimming on the water's surface isn't an issue for me either, and I'll happily swim lengths of a swimming pool. I do fear going underwater, though, and being submerged in a vast body of water would really take me out of my comfort zone.

After addressing these matters to the summer camp director, I get a reply stating that this is an instant deal-breaker because all of the international staff must be lifeguard certified. So, the search for the perfect summer camp continues.

Getting to work in America isn't the only challenge I have facing me. I'm also determined to pass my driving test before I leave England. I started taking driving lessons in June. Since then, I've had a continuous cycle of twice-weekly lessons that last up to two hours. By this point, I'm starting to grasp the basic driving skills of clutch control and gear changes.

Despite my delay in sitting in the driver's seat, I now want to drive a car. I want to have more freedom. I feel restricted from doing the many things that a typical 20-something year old does. I also want to increase my independence and feel like I'm growing up more and not lingering around the town that I've always lived in. This has also been a pivotal factor in my decision to travel and live *across the pond* on my own for a few months.

4

THE BIRTHDAY

It's now reached bonfire night, the night of my birthday. It seems like birthdays have become less special, compared to the celebrations I had in my teens and childhood. I guess that's what happens when you enter your twenties and life becomes more hectic and serious. As a family, we still do our annual celebrations on the day with garden fireworks. Most of these fireworks surge up like fountains, reaching the height of the garden fence. They rise with a racket, and I've never really trusted any of them to light up safely. They still bring me some happiness, though, as we watch with interest as a family.

It's the same process every year. Dad has a wheelbarrow ready, filled with sand for the fireworks to be propped in, and a glass bottle to prop up the rockets. Dad uses a flint to light up the fireworks, and once they're lit and fizzling, he'll hear the urgent calls from me and Mum, 15 yards behind him.

"Come on, Dad, get over here! Quick!" I shout.

We've had some accidents in the past on this day. They're comical, as I think back now. One incident involved a fallen firework that fired toward us on the garden patio. We repeatedly jumped up, as if we were playing the "double Dutch" game. Only this wasn't with skipping ropes. This was more dangerous, to avoid making contact from the fireworks.

Another incident involved a Catherine wheel, setting fire to one of the fence panels, which was quickly put out with a wet tea towel from the kitchen. There was also a rocket that hit a bedroom window, three doors down the road. Fortunately, no harm has befallen any living thing, although the cats scurry away in trepidation.

Some fireworks are disappointing and only last a few seconds. Others are unexpectedly loud and crackly. The rockets soar up to the stars with a high-pitched squeal, and then have the lamest climax with a quiet popping noise, and no color. But the unexpectedness of these low-quality fireworks from Sainsbury's still builds up our excitement on the night.

Once the fireworks are over, we have a nice dinner, followed by birthday cake and then the cards and presents are opened. They're nice evenings, even when they're on a weekday. And I notoriously get drunk on the closest weekend with my mates.

After my birthday, the wheels go back into motion, and I complete the first of many forms and fees for the Wild Packs recruitment agency. The first issue of forms includes my acceptance to the terms and conditions of the Wild Packs program. A copy of my passport is also needed.

In addition to this, I'm required to obtain two references from individuals who have supervised, taught, or employed me in the past. This is to provide an insight into the experience, skills, and personal qualities that I possess. I manage to get a former college teacher and university lecturer to provide me with references. I'm pleased to see that both of these people provide a satisfying review about me, boosting my self-esteem.

I also pay 35 pounds for a police check, which is processed by the Disclosure and Barring Service (DBS), once my application is sorted. My certificate of no criminal history, as well as my references, will ultimately determine my suitability and fittingness for a summer camp program.

5

A NEW OPPORTUNITY

In the second week of December, I get a call from Steph, a member of Wild Packs.

"Our agency likes what you've put in your application, George, so we decided to send it off to a camp yesterday. The director has responded to say that he is interested in having a chat with you. Is that okay?" Steph asks.

I'm pleased to hear that the agency thinks highly of my application. I'm also surprised at how they've found me another summer camp so fast.

"Yes, definitely. I'll look forward to receiving an email from them," I respond.

Steph tells me the name of the camp, and that she's going to send me the link to their website.

"The camp is a large, co-ed, traditional sports camp in New York state, and the director's name is Alex. Keep your eyes peeled for an email from him," Steph adds.

I'm instantly excited to hear that the camp is located near New York City, arguably the most popular tourist destination in America. On that same day, I receive an email from Alex, who tells me that he's intrigued by certain aspects of my application. He believes that I could be a *"great fit"* at his camp and specifies that he's usually free between 10 a.m. and 4 p.m. Eastern Standard Time (EST) and can also find time on the weekends for a Skype chat.

On a Sunday at 3 p.m. UK time, I ask Alex if he's available to talk. He quickly responds with his approval and gives me his Skype username so we can talk that night. He ends the email with the words, *in Friendship, Love and Spirit, Alex.* I think that this is a bizarre way to finish an email. Maybe it's a religious phrase or a term of endearment he uses—or maybe it's the type of language he uses at his summer camp. But I'm still willing to talk with him about a possible position because it seems more like a down to earth and *there for the children to have fun* kind of camp.

At 6:07 p.m., my request to add Alex on Skype is accepted and I then get ahold of Alex. Before the chat starts, I can see a frowning, almost disgusted look on his face. I ask Alex how his day has been.

"It could be better, George. It's bitterly cold here at the moment, and we've been hit by a snow blizzard, so I'm trying to keep warm in my office, talking to you."

It turns out that the northeastern part of the United States has been hit by a major winter storm, with over 20 inches of snowfall.

"Thousands of flights will be canceled because of this, and the New York and New Jersey governors have already declared a state of emergency, urging people to stay indoors. It's not good here at the moment, George."

I understood that the weather is making Alex feel deflated, yet it's disappointing for me to be approached like this. This chat ends up being similar to the first interview I had with Mike, though this time the interviewer appears less interested in what I have to say.

After I talk a little about my background and what job I'm currently doing, Alex then asks: "Can you give me a time in your life of when you acted as a leader?"

This is a question that I've thought about in depth. I remember a good example from college.

"During my sports degree at college, I was assessed on organizing and leading a basketball session for the other students on the course. I planned what drills I was going to teach them beforehand. I made sure a risk assessment was done and the right equipment was going to be used to ensure the session was delivered safely. I made sure there was a warm-up and cool-down, with stretches, to prevent injury. I also gave words of encouragement to the participants and everyone seemed to enjoy the session I delivered."

"Okay, cool," Alex says bluntly.

Another question he asks is: "What does it take for someone to be a good role model?"

I feel relieved, as this is another question that I've reflected on thoroughly, especially after my failure to answer it properly in my first interview. With Mike, this question left me puzzled as my mind drew a blank.

"Being inspiring...and err...being good at supervising children," I said to Mike without conviction. This time I know exactly what I wanted to say, as it also relates to my *employability strengths*.

"A role model needs to have passion and the ability to inspire others. They need to have selflessness and be able to accept others, no matter how different they are. And they also need to have the ability to overcome obstacles. Teamwork can overcome obstacles and bring success, and this message can be passed on to children from a role model."

Poker-faced Alex gives a few nods of approval, and I take that to be positive, considering the generally low mood that I perceive on the screen. Following on from this, Alex asks me if I have any queries for him. Out of courtesy, and to show interest, I ask him some general questions about what the daily routine is like at his camp. After all, it increases my knowledge of what to expect from a summer camp.

Alex ends the interview after only 20 minutes, as he has other interviews to complete. He tells me that he'll get in touch after Christmas and will let me know whether I'm considered for a job as a general counselor at his summer camp.

6

CHRISTMAS TIME

While I'm checking through my emails over the Christmas holiday, I discover that Wild Packs has closed their office and won't be officially reopening until January the 5th. I'm still waiting to hear if I'm in contention for a role within Alex's summer camp, although my first impression of him will leave me hesitant to accept any offer. My quest for a position at a summer camp is put aside for the time being, though. It's now Christmas and more family time.

Dad has a short time off his busy schedule as a self-employed builder, which he's continued since he was 17. He's bent over backwards to get jobs done, such as rebuilding brick walls and constructing patios in people's drives, in a matter of weeks. I've never heard about him disappointing anyone and loyal customers are lined up for his services. His long waiting list is due to his impeccable work ethic and civility, which is evident when I've worked with him on the rare occasion for extra cash.

The house phone rings regularly in the evening, disturbing Dad from his dinner. It's often someone requesting a building job to be done. Other times, it'll be phone calls from pigeon fanciers. He's kept pigeons all his life. It's a hobby that's been passed down by previous generations.

I can tell that Dad hopes one of his boys will continue his legacy of pigeon keeping, but we're reluctant to do so.

They aren't racing pigeons, as most people think. They're *exhibition birds*, as Dad likes to call them. They're shown in pens within venue halls or enormous tents at agricultural events. The criteria they're judged on include their feather quality and they must also have an upright, alert and confident stance inside the pen. Dad goes everywhere around the country with his pigeons—and Mum joins him for the company, but not out of choice.

There's a row of wooden lofts in the garden where the pigeons live. Within these lofts, Dad manages the birds in his own special way. He uses a scraper on the perches to remove the unpleasant coating of bird droppings and regularly changes the sawdust to maintain a level of cleanliness. Each loft contains a plastic feeder for water and another feeder for a mixture of grains, which are filled twice a day (before and after his work). The type of grains in this mixture include; maize, legumes and tic beans—providing a good source of protein to enable pigeon growth (from tiny squabs to *show quality* pigeons) and carbohydrate and fats to keep their bodies warm and supply them with energy. There are also steel trays, which Dad sporadically fills with water, which the birds use to bathe and preen their feathers in, keeping them clean and in order.

Dad has been very successful with his hobby over the years, winning rosettes and trophies for "the best in show" pigeon and featuring in many articles in the *Feathered World* magazine. His, and sometimes Mum's face, are printed in the papers for all the pigeon fanciers around the country to see. Dad's pigeon management even featured in a YouTube video recently. This was a surreal moment, to see cameras directing their attention to him in the garden while he was being interviewed. It was on a Sunday morning, and I had to look twice when I saw the interview out of the window, and not just because of being hungover from the night before.

In spite of teasing Dad for his repetitive and somewhat old-fashioned lifestyle for this day and age, he's the most reliable and hardworking person I know. These are qualities that everyone appreciates about him. They're also qualities that have made him very successful at what he does, as well as being the breadwinner of our family. And regardless of our wishes to miraculously have increased wealth and fortune one day, Dad has a frank but rational viewpoint in response:

"At the end of the day, some people are born rich, and some people are not born rich. You just have to make the best of what you've got."

Mum has helped provide a happy home for my brothers and me in all the years we've lived together. She has done most of the housework and cooking that *we men* take for granted. On top of that, Mum has a part-time job, being a dinner lady in a primary school. And as Mum comes from a Catholic background, we boys have been brought up into the faith, and have turned to God to give us strength, especially when life gets challenging.

I feel like Chris and I have modeled ourselves on Dad's hard work and commitment, and the kindhearted side of Mum, with everything we do. Chris shows this through his attentiveness in dealing with all the customer needs and problems in his service advisor role of our local supermarket.

This isn't to say that Tom isn't a caring and hardworking person. But he's left his cares behind in England to travel around the world. He doesn't regret this. He's already encountered many fantastic adventures and updates us on all the great friends he's made. Tom has also said some meaningful words to me before he left England that have helped inspire me to take on a new challenge in America.

"Do what *you* want to do, mate... Traveling will give you so much more confidence and a better perspective on life."

Tom is more of an extrovert, who always seems to be up for a challenge, which is why he worked for prosperous businesses in London. He's been employed as a salesman for events management organizations in the past. It required him to negotiate the selling and ordering of products that were marketed for exhibition venues—working under pressure with confidence and poise. He was proud to tell us about the number of sales he made, or when he's been awarded "salesman of the month." He then left all that behind to spend nine months in Australia, a couple of years ago.

Presently, he's traveling on a two-year working visa around New Zealand. The deep water and the highest of heights don't faze him, which is why he's participated in many extreme activities in his traveling history so far. This has included; scuba diving in Thailand, surfing at Agnes Water in Australia, exploring glowworm caves, and going white-water rafting down a waterfall in the Kawarau River, New Zealand. For his next adventure, he plans to go hiking on a glacier on the west coast of the South Island, New Zealand.

For now, though, it's time to celebrate Christmas with Mum, Dad, Chris and with the company of Rosie—our friendly, chubby, tabby cat. We hope Tom continues to have a brilliant time on the other side of the world.

7

THE UNCERTAINTY

I receive a call from Wild Packs. Unfortunately, it's bad news. Heather confirms that Alex hasn't selected me for this year's summer camp. I express my disappointment.

"Well, why didn't he tell me this? I've wanted to know the verdict for the last couple of weeks, so I can take action based on his decision."

"I understand that you're disappointed about this, and we're actually frustrated with the camp director about the way he's acted over this," Heather sympathizes.

"Is it too late for me to be accepted by a summer camp?" I ask.

Heather responds confidently, "You're definitely not too late, George. These next couple of months is when most summer camps start searching for employees, and when many candidates will be starting to fill out their applications."

I feel reassured to be told that I still have plenty of time to be recruited by a summer camp, yet the pendulum is swinging between good news and bad news. I'm uncertain of what's around the corner. Not only is the stress starting to show with the situation of the coming summer, but also with my driving progress. Peter is my driving instructor, who's always honest and gives me constructive criticism for essential skills, such as the "mirror, signal, maneuver" routine. I'm encouraged to take a practical test. I'm beginning to demonstrate signs of being a good driver, and he's beginning to show real optimism in me passing the test.

Despite this positivity emerging, I feel that I've put myself under the demand of too many things: playing for my local football team, meeting all the objectives in my current job, passing my driving test, and getting the ideal summer job in America. They've built up a lot of stress for me and it's led to me experiencing a panic attack. This is a new and very personal obstacle to overcome. The panic attacks are unsettling and I understand it's self-inflicted—caused by the commitments that are on my terms. The few times they've occurred have been on a Sunday, following the Friday and Saturday nights of drinking with my friends.

Stopping the drinking is part of the solution to the problem. I know this, and Mum reiterates it. But I enjoy going out and having drinks with my friends. I feel like I've earned these moments. Moments of drunkenness with friends are moments of freedom. They can be the only time I can really take my mind off the things that are stressing me out. There are exchanges in banter as the alcoholic beverages flow within my group. We often boast about how dominant our football teams are doing in the league and occasionally some flirting with girls occurs, as confidence creeps into our alcohol-fueled selves.

On rare occasions, those who are single may sacrifice a night out and, instead, meet up with a girl who's matched from the dating app, Tinder, installed on the phone. Tinder is used partly through boredom and partly in the faint hope of maybe, just maybe, meeting *the one*. Tinder is a funny invention, really. Not in the humorous sense, but in the perplexing sense. I feel that it's affecting humanity. The fact that people can now pick whom they want to date—or only going as far as one-night stands—with the decisive swipe of a finger is crazy. It's taken away the sacredness of what love used to be.

While there are some cases of Tinder working for people's relationships and marriages, many users of the app treat other people like pieces of meat in the supermarket, and judging people before ever meeting them in the flesh. Whatever happened to the good old-fashioned *bumping into someone in the pub and hitting it off* approach?

Regardless of the drinking habits with mates, though, my nights out in recent weeks have been tainted by *suffering Sundays*. I use this term because it's the day that my symptoms of anxiety worsens—once reality sets in again. I become fidgety and breathless while I try to function on a task in hand, and, at the same time, endure the hangover from Saturday night.

These symptoms are short-lived and ease away and thankfully my anxiety has never affected me to the point of taking time off work. Anxiety and alcohol, however, are shadows in my current journey. Although others have been defeated by them, fortunately I haven't.

8

AN IDEAL CAMP

It's now the middle of February, and I receive another email from a new summer camp director. This summer camp really catches my eye. The program director, Brandon, belongs to a YMCA camp located about an hour away from Chicago. YMCA stands for Young Men's Christian Association—a charitable organization that aims to inspire young people to reach their full potentials. This particular camp specializes in providing a summer of fun for campers with spina bifida. In my present job, I've worked with several young people who have spina bifida, so it's likely that I'll be familiar with the support and guidance that needs to be offered for these campers.

Brandon informs me in his email that the camp welcomes 16-20 campers each week, which are integrated into the residential camp with the other existing campers, totaling approximately 150 campers weekly. Brandon informs me that the campers may need assistance during their stay at camp, which can consist of various daily life tasks that able-bodied people take for granted. These tasks can involve; supporting a camper onto a shower seat, helping a camper to get dressed, or just simply tying a camper's shoelaces. Brandon adds that some campers will need no help whatsoever. It just depends on which kids attend the summer camp, and my comfort zone as a staff member in assisting them.

The campsite holds a 45-person counselor team, and there's always somebody to hang out with. And the facilities within Brandon's summer camp include an indoor swimming pool and a high ropes course with zip lines.

Brandon's first summer camp experience was working at this exact camp. A large part of his first summer was spent with a child who only needed help putting his shoes on, though Brandon used his extra availability to help with the needs of other campers. In his view, it was a very rewarding experience, but also a team effort. That's exactly how I feel about my job in England.

At the residential school, there's always a responsibility that you're obliged to help with. Sometimes I assist in transferring a wheelchair student into a standing frame, or onto a tricycle for a physiotherapy session. Meanwhile, other staff members will be supporting the learning needs of students in a classroom lesson. Sometimes, you need to set up and support a student with their communication aid in the classroom. One communication aid that's often used is called an augmentative-alternative communication (AAC) device. This is a computer device that allows an individual with severe speech impairment to have a voice and emit words out of the screen by pressing buttons.

There are also many responsibilities in the residential houses that are located on the school's campus. These duties can include feeding students with soft foods at mealtime if they have swallowing difficulties and assisting with personal care, in a dignified way. Sometimes, the needs of the children cannot be fulfilled by one staff member. Sometimes, the responsibilities require the support of specialist staff.

The delightful nature of the staff at this remarkable residential school, and the freedom and opportunities available to the students has enabled the children to live life to the fullest. We take pride in a child's achievements, and how they can see past their so-called limitations. They know they have much to offer, regardless of how restrictive their bodies might be. It's wonderful to see students enjoying life on the campus and moving through the corridors in their wheelchairs with beaming smiles, as they say hello to you. This is why I love my job.

The number of staff employed at the residential school is vast, and staff members are grouped into different networks. There are teachers, physiotherapists, speech and language therapists, occupational therapists, and student support assistants. Every staff member in my position must complete their objectives each day, for the benefit of the students, and we rely on camaraderie and collaboration in our multidisciplinary team approach.

I feel like fate has connected me with this camp and they can appreciate the experience I have. After reading Brandon's email, I promptly let him know that I'm extremely interested in his summer camp and what it offers to children with spina bifida.

Once I've exchanged Skype usernames with Brandon and arranged a time to talk, I give myself time to prepare for the interview. During my preparation, I research, in more depth, the condition of spina bifida. I then recall a few examples, from my own experience, of when a child's independence has been enabled, through simple and effective intervention. I also research the main objectives of Brandon's camp.

I then make a visual and verbal connection with Brandon on the laptop screen. After being greeted by Brandon and after telling him a bit more about myself, I'm asked what I know about individuals with spina bifida. From personal knowledge and what I've researched, spina bifida means a "split or open spine." The spinal column of a fetus doesn't close all the way and this can damage the nerves that run through the spinal cord. As a result, it can cause muscle weakness, or paralysis of the body below the opening. In the most severe cases, many individuals can be unable to walk, and may have bladder and bowel related issues.

Brandon goes on to ask the predictable question of why I'm interested in his summer camp. I respond by saying that it appears to be a great place for campers to make friends because they can meet other individuals who they can relate to. I add that it also appears to be a place that allows individuals to achieve more because at this camp they can do things they thought they couldn't. This can generate new hobbies for them. For instance, the children can get a motivational boost after using the high ropes and zip line facilities, and this can become an outdoor activity for them and their family.

"That's very true, George. It's also a place that teaches every child how to be more independent after camp. And I'm sure the parents and children at the school you work at can see developments in this area too."

I then say that one of the most important aims in my job is to develop a child's self-reliance. I always aim to get the best out of the children, whether it's in the classroom doing school work, supporting them in the swimming pool, or guiding them through their participation in other sport and leisure activities. I also encourage the students to partake in activities of daily living in their shared accommodations, to enable them to become more independent.

By the end of the interview, Brandon seems impressed with the knowledge and experience that I've shared. I cannot see myself being rejected this time.

Heather from Wild Packs calls me the next day asking how the interview went and is pleased to hear that I've got high hopes.

"I've got my fingers crossed that it works out for you. If you could let me know once you've heard something, that would be great," Heather says before we end the call.

After waiting a week for Brandon's verdict, I receive an email from Heather again. I cannot believe my eyes. Heather's email reads that she heard back from Brandon, and, unfortunately, the camp isn't able to offer me a contract for this summer. Heather seems to think that there's a problem with their budget, rather than the interview. I sink into my sofa at home, in despair. More time has been wasted.

I question whether I should make myself available again for the selection process. What if it's only going to lead to further refusal from a summer camp director? Heather can understand my skepticism, yet she assures me that the Wild Packs team will go back to the drawing board and will look for alternative placements.

9

ONE MORE CHANCE

It's the beginning of March and I've booked my practical driving test, which is scheduled for next month. I'm still making mistakes in my lessons, yet these mistakes are occurring less often of late and my confidence as a learner driver is growing.

With that said, I call the ever-reliable Wild Packs on the phone, and a man called Russell answers. I inform Russell that I'm considering giving up the search for a summer camp. Having reached no agreement with a summer camp director yet is discouraging for me. Russell has already learned from his colleagues about the complications I've experienced and proposes an idea to me.

"There is a camp that I was a general counselor for in North Pennsylvania, called Camp Ace Invaders. I spent a summer there, and loved it. I know you've faced a few rejections from other places, but the head staff members at this camp are a friendly bunch. All you need to do is fill out their application form, which is found on their website, and they will get back to you."

Russell motivates me to apply for this summer camp. After the phone call, I complete the application form that he told me about. Later that same day, I'm contacted by Camp Ace Invaders in an email. I'm informed that my application is going to be reviewed, and that I'll be contacted if a position is available that matches my preferences.

Roughly an hour after this email, I received another one from the very same camp. This time the email is sent directly from a man, named Bobby. He reviewed my application and would love to get a chance to organize an interview on Skype or FaceTime. Bobby wants to learn more about my personal qualifications and discuss my interest in joining the staff at Camp Ace Invaders for the upcoming summer. He leaves the ball in my court and allows me to decide the best day and best times for an interview, working around my schedule. The sincerity and genuine interest in Bobby's email pleases me. Once again, I'm hopeful of becoming an international worker in America.

After I organize my chat for a possible position among the staff at Camp Ace Invaders, I then realize that I've become reliant on Skype. I've known of its existence for a while, and I know many people that are using it, but I've never had to use it in the past. In the last six months, however, Skype has become a necessary resource in my search for work at an American summer camp. This is what our society has become. Society is forcing us to modernize, to change the way we live and become associated with the world's latest creations. In our current state, where people are constantly glued to the "apps" installed on their phones, we must conform through social media trends.

Time flashes by, and it's an hour before the interview with Bobby. I prepare myself in the same fashion as before. I briefly research the summer camp in question, to learn about the positive vibes that they promote online. I also reanalyze the questions I've already encountered in previous interviews, reflecting on the answers that I've given. I also write some of my thoughts on paper as I believe this will present more clarity in what I'm saying out loud to the summer camp director.

At 1 p.m. I video call Bobby on his username. He answers the call. The picture on my screen presents a man with a red baseball cap and in a navy t-shirt with the camp's logo on it. He has piercing blue eyes, like mine, that are seen through the lenses of his glasses. As we start talking, I'm put at ease by Bobby, who seems to be as genuine as he was in the emails we exchanged beforehand. The interview moves on to my life and my occupation, which Bobby thinks is really admirable. One comment from him will stick in my head forever, though.

"I know it's a rewarding job, and I get that it must be a tiring job for you, George, to help look after so many children in the school and the residential home. But I personally believe that working at Camp Ace Invaders will be *the hardest job that you'll love.*"

I can't comprehend that comment at the time. How could it be such a great job, if it would be the hardest job I'll experience? What makes it so enjoyable? I realize that I'd never understand this message from Bobby unless I became a general counselor and embark on a summer at Camp Ace Invaders.

Bobby then asks me what I know about his camp. I say (stating the obvious) that the campsite presents a safe and positive place for the campers, which allows them to have lots of fun. I also say how stunning the campus looks on the website.

"Yeah, the campus is really great, and spans over 180 acres in northeastern Pennsylvania. We do so many sports and activities across i all. You name a sport, and we play it. And Maple Lagoon is beautiful and a key landmark for the camp. It's used as a safe waterfront for all the water sports," Bobby says.

This captivates me and I'm more interested about getting a position there. Bobby then asks me what age groups I have the most experience working with in England. I tell him that I currently work with 12- to 18-year-old students at the school, but I'm sometimes assigned to younger age groups, depending on staffing numbers. Bobby is jotting things down on his notepad after my responses, which is probably going to be used to give the management team an idea about me. Bobby then goes on to discuss the campers.

"You'll get a big mixture of campers at Camp Ace Invaders, depending on which age division you're selected for. You'll be working with the nicest kids in the world, but then you'll also have the brattiest and most immature of campers. Most of the campers come from Jewish backgrounds. And many parents work high-salary occupations, so the children are often brought up in a comfortable lifestyle, and many of them have been able to get away with behavior that's unacceptable at our camp. It will be your responsibility, along with the other counselors, to make sure everyone is keeping with the rules and regulations, which includes making their beds every morning. And in addition to promoting good behavior, you'll be making sure the campers are living in a fun and safe environment."

I ensure Bobby that I'll do my utmost to achieve these responsibilities. But I'm a bit concerned by the insight into the summer camp lifestyle. How much pressure will I be put under when supervising the children I'll be working with? Sometimes children at the school have behavior that's unacceptable, but it's not just my responsibility to deal with this. The teachers, residential staff, and the safeguarding officer also have the responsibility of managing a child's behavior. In the summer camp, however, it's likely that I'll have limited support in reducing any undesired behavior from a child.

Nevertheless, I'm still thinking positively. I've already perceived Bobby to be a well-informed man, who's reassured me by answering my early concerns. Bobby tells me that the summer camp experience will last eight weeks, which includes the orientation week—meaning that I'll have a month of traveling to enjoy after my employment. Bobby adds that I'll have a few evenings free, where I'll be able to socialize with other staff at camp, instead of overnight duties with the children. Counselors are also allowed a total of six days off throughout the summer to have a break away from the hustle and bustle of camp. These off-duties will also provide the opportunity to contact friends and family on Skype and Facebook. Each counselor gets the opportunity to use two of their days off for overnight stays elsewhere, of their own choosing and expenditure. This must be approved at least one week in advance by a head counselor. Bobby then brings me other satisfying news.

"We have the luxury this year of securing our counselors' lounge which has free Wi-Fi, so you'll have unlimited use of the Internet when you're not working. There will also be five accessible computers if you don't have your own devices with you," Bobby says.

This makes me wonder how the staff members from previous years have coped with less access to social media. Did having no internet make it a disappointing experience? Maybe that's why this new technological intervention has been made.

"It's been a pleasure getting to know you more, George. Thank you for your time to talk with me today. I'll forward your feedback to Vince, who's the camp's owner and director, and we'll discuss the arrangements for a second interview with you to secure a position for this summer," Bobby concludes.

I thank Bobby for his time, and I begin to feel confident, that this application will be the one that rewards me with a place at a summer camp. If I believed in fate, I would think that we were destined to meet.

10

THE BIG TALK

Within a week, I receive the email that I've been waiting for from Vince, the director of Camp Ace Invaders. Vince indicates in his email that he was suggested, by Bobby, to reach out and discuss a potential role with me at his summer camp. Through prompt exchanges in emails, we arrange to have a Skype chat the next evening, after I finish work.

When the next day comes, all I'm thinking about is the evening call that's looming. I must make an outstanding impression on Vince because I count this Skype conversation as my last chance of becoming an international worker in America. Anymore disappointing news from a camp and I'll call it quits.

I keep my composure and finish my day at work. After walking back home, I then go onto my laptop to analyze the literature on the Camp Ace Invaders website. I write down words that catch my eye, and that I think will catch the attention of Vince. Preparing for these interviews has somewhat reminded me of my days as a student at college and university, when I used my researching skills to investigate and gather relevant literature for the chosen assignment. Notes I've made are fresh in my head after reading them back.

I glance at the clock, and as the last minutes agonizingly tick by, it gets to 6 p.m. It's only a matter of time until Vince is going to call me. This is the same man that I saw on the summer camp's promotional video. In that video, Vince appears very welcoming toward people, like me, who are applying to work at Camp Ace Invaders.

Then the jingle of the Skype call alarms me in the room, and it rattles my nerves. I press the video call icon, and there's Vince.

After seeing this authoritative figure on my laptop screen, there's a tense pause. We then say hello and, unlike Bobby, Vince approaches this conversation with a more serious demeanor.

"Although it will seem like a fun and happy place for the kids, the standards are very high at this camp, from the soccer and basketball specialists, to all the general counselors who live with the kids. We only hire *the best* people for the job. One of your main aims will be to increase the self-confidence of each of the campers you're assigned to, so that they go home feeling more self-assured, that they have done this whole experience by themselves. If they've enjoyed their experience, it will make them and their families want to come back to us again. This can only be achieved by you."

Vince's words make complete sense. He puts into perspective the fact that there'll be children who'll spend most of their two months with me this summer. Therefore, I'll be the one who determines how amazing their summer will be. If a child goes home upset and says that they didn't love their summer, then their family won't bring them back again. From a business viewpoint, the camp will lose out on income from that kid next summer.

"Children will get homesick. You will have children in your bunkhouse that will be homesick. So, when a kid comes up to you and says they're homesick and want to go home, what will you do?"

This leads to a couple of nervy seconds before I speak.

"If a kid is homesick, they're probably not having enough fun, so I'll try to take their mind off it by playing games and encourage them to socialize with their bunkmates."

"What if they don't want to play a game? As a role model to the kids, you've got to show that you care, and reassure them," Vince says.

"I'll do my utmost to reassure them by listening and empathizing with them. There was a time when I was homesick during a week-long trip away. I was only about eight and was out with the cubs and scouts. hated the first couple of days and cried. But the more I took part in activities with the other cubs and scouts, the more I enjoyed myself. And I didn't want to leave by the end. Maybe I can add this into the chat."

Vince replies, "Yes, that's exactly what you should talk about to your homesick children. They'll think more of you as a role model if they know that you once struggled with homesickness and overcame it."

I begin to feel more at ease because I can sense that Vince appreciated my answer—nonetheless, I'm still alert to the challenging questions that Vince will undoubtedly spring upon me.

"So, George, because the campers don't have their mums or dad with them, they will all navigate friendships with their campers and counselors, to help them get through their summers. In order for you to have good relationships with the campers, it's not just about helping them have fun playing soccer, basketball, or jumping into the water. It's about allowing them to become more independent and making them feel empowered. How can you make this happen?"

This again causes me to pause for a few seconds to register what the thought-provoking question means. I have to think logically once more.

"If I relate it to my current job, one way of gaining a child's independence is by setting them jobs. For example, I may ask them to photocopy worksheets for a lesson, or to choose a book from the library that I will read to the group."

Vince sharply responds, "That's all well and good to give them chores to do, to make them more independent. Our camp aims to do that anyway, with the clean-ups and inspections we do every day. How about when you're out on activities with them, and some of your kids don't want to do an activity because they've never tried it, or they may not think that it's safe enough?"

Another light bulb goes off in my head.

"I won't just encourage the campers to partake in activities that they aren't familiar with; I'll also try all the activities myself, to show that I'm willing to try new things. Hopefully, that will give them the confidence to do the same."

Vince gives me a nod of approval. Quiet contentment radiates off him. It's now time for me to ask any questions I might have.

Among the responses to the generalized questions that I ask, Vince informs me that all of the information will be in the manual booklet that I'll receive if I'm awarded a position with Camp Ace Invaders. I then ask Vince what the situation is regarding time away from the campsite in the evening, and he gives me a strict overview.

"You will be on a rota with other counselors where you will have your own nights to stay with the campers who belong in your cabin. This is what we call an OD, which means on-duty in *summer camp language*. What you do when you're not on an OD is up to you, as long as you follow the camp rules and regulations. These include making sure you return to camp and sign yourself in before 12.30 a.m. When you're off-site, you need to make sure you're not in a drunk or disorderly condition that prevents you from interacting with your kids in the night if they ever need anything. Failure to not obey the rules or curfew can result in extra ODs, a loss of a day off, or potential termination."

Alcohol consumption has been a regular weekend occurrence for me, and (up until now) I've probably been a borderline binge drinker, if I'm brutally honest. Of course, I'll have a drink on the occasional night off at the summer camp, but I must remain level-headed, too.

When the interview is finished, I'm relieved to have broken the ice with the camp's director—though now I'm anxiously hoping that Vince will bring me the wonderful news of welcoming me on board.

11

THE DELIGHT

A day later, I get an email from Vince.

"Consider this your official welcome to the Ace Invaders family for summer 2015!"

I fist pump the air in delight. I then run out of my bedroom and downstairs to tell the news to my family, like a big kid. It makes me realize the importance of perseverance and determination when you want to achieve something.

My last act of perseverance was when I managed to raise 2,000 pounds for homelessness, with a friend from university, by doing a grueling sponsored walk. We aimed to visit many professional football stadiums in the south of England, and, in return, we gained prodigious attention from local newspapers and radio stations and received signed memorabilia from famous football clubs, which we auctioned and put toward our fundraising total.

Unfortunately, I came up short of the 250-mile target, and was escorted by my friend and a Good Samaritan to the nearest emergency department with badly blistered feet at the 100-mile mark. That was my fault for wearing brand new trainers, as opposed to worn-in shoes that fit the feet better. But we're still very proud of our efforts, and it didn't stop me from visiting more stadiums with my friend a few days later with the help of public transport!

The fantastic news of today has revealed that traveling to America is my destiny after all. It'll actually be happening this summer! Vince's email is my key to the door of acceptance at an American summer camp. His email also contains my contract that I'll sign and send them back, as well as my staff handbook. I can now use the handbook as an informational guide to many of my questions that may arise before I start at camp.

On the same day that I receive the terrific news from Vince, I also receive a celebratory email from Cameron at Wild Packs, for being accepted at a summer camp. The email also urgently suggests that I better *"get moving"* by collating all the paperwork I need before I can apply for my visa. This paperwork is all to be found in my Wild Packs account.

"Give me a chance," I mutter to myself.

The additional information in Cameron's email consists of the balance of my fees that are now due. For first-timers, like me, the joining on fee is £285 (or $400). I'm a little taken back by this. I knew that I have to make payments in preparation for my trip, in addition to the return flights, but I thought that they'd all be small payments, such as the DBS check that I've already paid.

A couple of days later, during my lunchbreak at work, my phone starts ringing. It's an unknown number. Usually, an unknown caller means a cold call. Cold calling has become a common occurrence in recent years, especially on the house phone. It aggravates Mum and Dad who always answer, anticipating that it'll be a call for Dad about his pigeons or building work, or that it might be a friend or relative calling. Often, to our disgust, it's a foreign caller from a company that we've never heard of before. These so-called companies require a survey, or they advertise one of their products that they're aggressively selling. We've become susceptible to abruptly ending these conversations as soon as we understand the displeasing nature of these phone calls.

I answer my mobile phone this time, and it's Heather from Wild Packs. After I tell her that I got a position at Camp Ace Invaders, she congratulates me.

"I am genuinely really happy for you, George. I felt so bad about what happened with the last camp. You didn't deserve that at all, and it really made my day when I found out that you were successful at Camp Ace Invaders. For what it's worth, when I first started working for Wild Packs, Camp Ace Invaders was the one camp I always wanted to work at. So, I'm pretty sure you're in for a fabulous summer there."

This fills me with another buzz of excitement. I think that I've made a really good decision joining this camp, because Russell also gave the camp high approval. I have a lot of admiration for the Wild Packs team for doing their utmost in giving me a position at a summer camp. I make my gratitude known to Heather.

Heather and the optimism from the team at Wild Packs have been my doses of anesthesia that have helped me through the, *at times*, painful recruitment process. I appreciate the motivation they gave me to stay positive. They were certain that I'd get a placement somewhere, and thankfully it happened.

Heather then reiterates that I need to complete the agency's fees and paperwork before I can receive my visa paperwork.

"The sooner you get this done, George, the sooner we can get you planning your embassy visit," she adds.

Once I check my emails again, I notice that I've received an email from a lady called Michaela. She's from a company called Gap-Year-Express, which has a close relationship with Wild Packs. Michaela explains that she can sort out my flight and will know first-hand if any changes need to be made to my flight once it's processed. Cheap and flexible tickets are on the agenda.

Michaela then offers me the most cost-effective flight based on the details I gave her, which includes my preferred date of arrival at Scranton airport. Michaela's offer involves flying with American Airlines, which includes free Wi-Fi and power outlets to charge my phone and laptop. The flight package comes to £710 (or $996). I'm not sure if this is good value. I haven't done extensive research into the cheapest flight prices; nonetheless, I trust that Michaela will save me some money.

In the same email, Michaela requests that I provide her with my bank details. I'm skeptical about sharing bank details with companies that I've had no experience with. There's also been a scamming rise of late, however, I remember Wild Packs previously stating that they were in partnership with Gap-Year-Express and that their servers are 100% secured against fraudulent activity. I confirm the bank details to Michaela.

12

IN THE THICK OF IT

It's the end of March, and another significant priority is arranging an appointment at the U.S. embassy. Wild Packs will schedule my appointment in London. I've been notified by Gemma (from the agency) that a fee of £140 (or $196) has been added to my application, which is the cost for Wild Packs to book an embassy appointment. It cannot be booked until the fee is paid.

A non-immigrant visa application form (DS-160), is attached to Gemma's email, which asks for my program number. As stated on the email, it's vital to take my time and complete the DS-160 correctly, because if any of my input is incorrect on the form, then it could jeopardize my visa. The rest of the email contains information to support me in completing the form correctly.

Meanwhile, I reach an agreement on my return flights, which includes my departure from New York City in September. I specify to Michaela, before the official booking of my flight, that the 12th of September is the perfect date to depart back to England because it'll complete the three permissible months of my visa and will allow me to enjoy some traveling experience.

Now that Michaela has my confirmation, she goes ahead and tickets the flights. After the payment is processed, I'm swiftly issued with an E-ticket that I can access online, showing my flight itinerary and reservation number. That's one less job that needs doing—or so I think.

A couple of days later, I receive an email from Marie, the co-owner of Camp Ace Invaders and the wife of Vince. In the email, Marie introduces forms to me that need to be printed, filled out in pen, scanned, and then emailed back to either Vince or Marie. These forms include a physician's examination, to be completed by my doctor, and an immunization form that requires input from a nurse at the local health center.

That week I attend an appointment with the practice nurse in the clinic. They check what vaccinations I'm missing on my immunization form. They then boost me with the necessary injections, which include a combined Hepatitis A and B vaccination.

"Sharp scratch," says the nurse, before piercing my skin with each injection.

The next day at the health center, the doctor reviews my medical history and assesses my abdomen, heart rate and blood pressure that contribute to my general health. The doctor reveals to me that I have good health and certifies this on the physical examination form. After the appointment, I'm charged £50 for the 15 minutes spent with the doctor.

"Are you joking? That appointment can't be worth 50 quid," I say in resentment.

The receptionist looks back at me awkwardly. "I'm sorry, but that's the general rate we charge for appointments that are required for private companies, which includes the overseas summer camp you're going to," she replies.

I pay the fee, which was halved from £100, based on the shortness of the meeting. The scanned forms are then sent back to Marie.

I then start completing my DS-160 form with the support of a help sheet that Gemma attached to an email. Once this is sorted, I'm able to download my finalized embassy application, which I send back to Gemma.

Words are flying back and forth on emails, which leads to me having the occasional restless night in bed, overthinking the current obstacles in my way. Anything America-related has to now be put on hold, though, because, in the midst of all of this, I'm planning on passing my driving test. This is the next challenge I'll be facing.

13

THE DRIVING TEST

Its 20 minutes before the test is set to commence. After signing into the test center, I wait in silence with Peter, my driving instructor. There's another guy, who's waiting in equal anticipation with his mother. The silence only creates more anxiety.

Before I know it, I'm sitting my test, beside the assessor, who looks and sounds a lot like Squidward from *SpongeBob SquarePants*. I read out a number plate in the distance and answer a couple of vehicle safety questions correctly. I then pull away from the car park, and the car starts juddering. And I stall it. I hear a sigh of disappointment from the examiner. Not a good start.

As I start driving on the roads, I can hear the examiner's pen squiggling notes on the assessment paper, and I see his stone-face glaring at me in my peripheral vision, particularly when I'm turning at a junction, or approaching a roundabout. This only adds to my discontent in the car with him. I must avoid thinking about what could go wrong; such as hitting an elderly lady that's crossing the road with her walking frame, or knocking a cyclist off their bike.

At one particular stage of the test, I stop the car, on handbrake, and wait with unnecessary hesitation at a T-junction. I stopped, looking ahead at the calmness of the dual carriageway, until the assessor suddenly blared out:

"Are you going to go out then, or what?!"

My heart then races as I release the handbrake, cross the central reservation, and turn right onto the dual carriageway. I then accelerate the car until it almost goes beyond the national speed limit of 70 miles an hour, until I realize that I could be undertaking the car on my right if I continue.

This then leads onto my independent drive where I'm looking intently at the road signs, to match the examiner's directions, instead of the ideal scenario of getting out a sat-nav and flicking on cruise control. After reaching my destination and performing a three-point turn on a remote road, I return to the center with a successful bay park. The test is over. Most of it already feels like a blur to me and as soon as I turn the engine off, the assessor doesn't ask me how I thought it went. This surprises me.

"Do you want to bring your driving instructor over to the car, or shall we talk about it with him inside?" the assessor asks.

I anxiously gulp. I think that this question means bad news for me. I can see Peter in the distance. He's just outside the test center, looking over at me from the entrance. I poke my head out of the window and signal for Peter to come over.

When Peter walks over, the assessor turns away from his assessment paper with a look of disapproval.

"Well, you've passed," he says.

I look twice at the assessor, as I'm flabbergasted by the news. But I'm delighted inside. Before I can say anything, the grouchy assessor continues:

"You were very lucky, though. At one point I could've given you a major when you hesitated at making that turn at the T-junction."

"I understand," I replied.

I act as though I'm taking the analysis of the test seriously, yet all I want to do is celebrate. I can pinch myself and say that I passed my practical driving test. I overcame it with eight minors, which included; not pressing the clutch in time with a gear change, ignoring mirror checks at a junction, and stalling the car, of course.

However, this driving certificate that I've been awarded is another key that'll unlock the door to further independence in my life. It's another step to adulthood and will break up the monotony.

When Peter drives me back home, we're relaxed and speaking to each other in a friendly tone, in contrast to the formality I've experienced with him in the past. I'll never forget what Peter said to me in that conversation.

"I get great satisfaction out of my job as a driving instructor when I see people like you passing, because you've been nervous driving with me. But seeing a person like you do well…that makes me happy."

In the evening, I spontaneously decide to go out clubbing with a few mates from work, to rejoice in my success. It's the weekend tomorrow, so a hangover won't be disastrous—maybe a hindrance to my performance in the fixture for my football team.

The next day (and with five hours sleep), my football team wins three-nil and it's especially pleasing for me to not concede a goal in defense. Chris's 27th birthday is tomorrow, so I go out with him and his mates—drinking two nights in a row.

On Sunday, I wake up with lightheadedness and it takes a while to realize what world I'm living in. I then walk downstairs, with red, glazed eyes, to find Chris lying on the sofa with last night's clothes still on. Once Chris wakes up, he gets the hangover giggles, as the alcohol in his blood gets brought back for a revival tour.

It doesn't take long for Mum to start nagging about why we got so drunk. And I know that it'll be irresponsible for me to drive a car in this state. The high numbers of drink-driving causalities, in the UK, highlight this to me.

We've arranged to speak with Tom after dinner and birthday cake. Tom's birthday is a day after Chris's, so Skype calling Tom this evening means that we'll be calling on the morning of his birthday, as there's a 12-hour difference between us and New Zealand.

When we get through to Tom and ask how he's been doing lately, he leaves us all slack-jawed with his latest activities. Most recently, Tom has accomplished a skydive of over 15,000 feet in Auckland. Tom said it was one of the most daring but enjoyable things he's ever experienced, with beautiful views that covered both the east and west coast of the North Island, in New Zealand.

Tom had his skydiving recorded by the company that he jumped with. It's on a CD ROM, and he'll be showing us how the whole day went when he returns to England. In addition to this, Tom also said that he's thinking of traveling over to East Asia once he has visited most of New Zealand. He hopes to do this in the next few months.

These are other examples that demonstrate Tom's pursuit of living life to the fullest. He always wants to experience different cultures and try new things, which has inspired me to take on an American adventure. After all, life's too short to stay in one place, especially if you're looking for a new adventure. There are a lot of places to explore in this world.

14

ANOTHER SETBACK

Gemma writes to me that she booked my American embassy appointment later this month, for the 23rd of April. I'm also relieved that I've finally broken the news to the school that I'll need to temporarily terminate my employment, so that I can depart to America in June. My line manager is happy to have me back under the same contract, which can be continued when I return in September.

Things seem rosy, until the unthinkable happens. I've brushed aside my flight tickets, but after reviewing them again, I realize that I'm going to be returning home in the WRONG MONTH! My hands freeze above the keyboard. I immediately ring Michaela in anguish, stating the mistake that was made on the tickets.

"So, what will happen to the changes now then? Will I get any money back? It's a lot of money for me to just throw away," I say.

"You won't get all of it back, as you will now have to pay a cancellation fee of approximately £300 because of the delayed changes you will have to make," Michaela replies.

I'm angered by this, and equally disappointed in myself for not paying attention to the flight details until it was too late. I also feel like

I'm right in blaming Michaela for her lapse in concentration toward my flight booking request.

"I will do my best to give you a cheap deal with the changes made and I will ask for your cancellation as quickly as possible," Michaela replies in a lowered voice. She can sense my grief.

"Make sure the return date is for September the 12th this time," I declare. Frustration burns within me as I disconnect the call.

Later, I open a confirmation email from Michaela. It's issued with an E-ticket now showing the correct dates and times for my arrival and departure. I reluctantly pay my cancellation fee of £300 in an online link in the email, taking the total to over £1000 for the return tickets. Even though this is unsettling to comprehend, I know that there's no other option but to pay the expense. I've come so far with organizing this working vacation that I should just take this mistake as part of the learning curve and move on.

With that said, it's undeniable that I'm mired in anxiety, and I can find it impossible to relax. The symptoms that I've been experiencing make it difficult to deny that it's not just a psychological issue, and that something might not be right physically. I get breathless with muscles in my arms and legs twitching, and I often feel dizzy and fatigued. These physical symptoms can be intensified by sleepless nights.

The next evening, after a busy day at work, I feel weak. I'm supposed to be going to football training, but I decide to not go because feel that it'll be too physically demanding in my current condition. A continuous cycle of juggling the commitments in my life has made my brain whirl, which becomes noticeable to Mum in particular.

Due to this, I decide to arrange a telephone counseling appointment that I heard about on the radio. This form of counseling is known as iTalk and is operated by the NHS. It's one of the recent services of the NHS, providing a short-term cognitive behavioral therapy program.

I believe that anxiety is underdiagnosed and undertreated by health care professionals. I addressed my symptoms during the physical examination with my doctor. In that short appointment I was told that my body is fine, even though it didn't feel like it was fine. They offered to send me away with a prescription for sertraline. I refused this and persevered.

It's refreshing to hear about this new service in the NHS that helps people who are challenged by anxiety and depression. I'm hoping that this can at least reduce the effects of this new bane in my life, so that I can continue my focus in preparing to go to America in June. Instead of feeling heavy and anxious, I want to feel weightless and fearless. I want to prepare for my adventure, without thinking that it's a bad idea. I want to be away from England, thinking that I've made the right decision.

15

THE EMBASSY

It's the day of the appointment at the American embassy. The sun is shining as I set off to get a train in the morning, starting from my hometown and going toward London Waterloo, and then getting an underground train to Bond Street. When I arrive at Bond Street Station, I use the Google Maps app on my phone to navigate me to the American embassy. During this eight-minute walk, I pass through some upmarket streets filled with business people. I feel very out of place in my blue-and-white striped polo shirt and khaki shorts. I'm carrying a rucksack, containing my passport and a confirmation form of my DS-160 application.

Eventually, I see a large, squared park. There's a lot more activity going on there, compared to these silent, albeit affluent, streets. I walk along the pavement of what I think leads me to one of the edges of Grosvenor Square. As I walk closer, I can now see that I'm a stone's throw away from the American embassy, a colossal block building with the U.S. flag protruding out from the top, and with a huge bald eagle sculpture just below that. There's a long line of people outside this building, and as I walk nearer, I realize that these people are just like me. They're waiting to enter the building for their appointments.

As I go to the end of the queue, I glance at my watch and its 11:15 a.m. I'm doing well with time, as my appointment is arranged for noon. I stand next to another guy who appears to be of a similar height to me of around six feet. But he has a black mop of curly hair, as opposed to my crewcut hair, styled with a wax product. We introduce ourselves to each other. His name is Fredric, and he's from Kent. He tells me that he's reapplying for a working visa to go back to Camp Ace Invaders.

"No way, I'm going there too!" I say in amazement.

Fredric goes on to tell me that he had experienced his first summer at the camp last year, when he was a specialist counselor in the media department. He used a professional camera on a regular basis to take pictures and videos of everyone getting involved in all the activities that the summer camp has to offer. His specialist team at the camp also regularly worked on the weekly newsletters that got sent to all the families, which promoted the entertainment that was relished by all the campers. Fredric also did some production work, such as light and sound checking for the live performances that occur in the sports hall during the evening shows. Many campers and counselors are involved in these shows over the course of the summer.

"You might be on stage this summer," laughs Fredric.

I laugh at the idea, as it seems unrealistic. I've never been an on stage performer before, apart from the minor parts I had in the school plays. But at least I can say I was one of the three wise men in a nativity, long ago.

Around 20 minutes later, we're near the front of the queue. I notice that most of the people around me, including Fredric, are holding their documents together. I get my documents out of my rucksack.

Moments after, Fredric walks over to the entrance of the building. One of the security guards then stops me in my tracks, and I wait for guards in front of me to finish scanning people's confirmation pages. When it's my turn, a lady asks for my DS-160 confirmation page, which should display my photo. My heart sinks. Although my confirmation page has a barcode and an application number to scan me through, the copy that I printed doesn't display my picture. A passport-style photo was uploaded during the completion of my application, yet this isn't visible in hard copy.

"This isn't the correct form. You need photographic evidence on it," a female organizer says.

"Can I still have my appointment today?" I respond.

"Yes. But you need to go to the print shop down Audley Road, directly behind you, where you can reprint a new confirmation page."

The lady gives me a business card that has the name of the print shop. I walk shamefully past the countless number of people who remain in the queue that I spent 30 minutes in.

I walk to the print shop with mixed emotions. I'm ticked off about making another mistake. The business card does slightly reassure me, though. But why did the lady have this card ready for me? Maybe other people have also had to reprint their confirmation page. I feel frustrated with the system. Completing the non-immigration visa has been a vexatious task from the start.

After I print a correct version of the confirmation page, it feels like "deja vu all over again," to quote Yogi Berra, as I approach the American embassy a second time. I look at my watch and it's just gone noon. I feel unsettled about entering the building late.

Fortunately, the length of the line is significantly reduced, and after 10 minutes, I'm one of the last people to be scanned through the first gate. Moments after being checked by the security guards, I find myself sitting in the waiting room, with a slip of paper that displays the number 612. I now wait until this number is called, so that I can be screened by one of the officers.

I look around the voluminous room. Most people are sitting and talking to each other. They appear to be in their late teens or early twenties, like me. I'm amazed by how much communication is going on. For many of the people talking to one another, it's probably the first time that they've met. I guess this shows that they're friendly and approachable people, which are the type of people that you need in a summer camp.

After 20 minutes, the number I was given on a slip of paper is called out by a lady in the organizing team. I enter what looks like a cashier booth that you'd see in a bank and I meet a consular officer. He asks for all the documentation that I've brought with me today.

The man scrutinizes the documents I give him. He then asks me personal questions, related to why I want to have a working visa in America.

"How long are you spending in America?" the officer asks.

"Three months," I reply.

"Where are you going to be working?" the man asks.

"At a summer camp in Pennsylvania," I reply.

"How are you going to spend the rest of your time in America?" the man asks.

"I'm going to be traveling in America for a month after I finish working at the summer camp," I reply.

A couple more intrusive questions follow. I reply to each question with honesty. The man then declares that the interview is over.

"Okay, you're free to go. Thank you and have a safe trip to America. You may leave the building through the exit doors on your left."

The man retains my passport. After leaving the embassy, I make use of my time in London and visit Oxford Street. I start window shopping, until I purchase a couple of CDs that I plan to listen to in my car. I later arrive at London Waterloo Station and treat myself to a McDonald's Big Mac meal before catching the next train ride home. I thought that this was a very American thing to do.

16

DEALING WITH WORRY

Fast forward three weeks, and I continue with my telephone counseling. I have a phone call from a lady called Sophie, once a week. This phone call occurs every Monday because that's the day I have my "twilight" shift at work, which begins in the late afternoon. This leaves the morning available for Sophie to contact me. The conversation normally lasts between 30-45 minutes and is entirely about me.

Sophie questions me about my concerns. She has been my mentor, who has helped me overcome doubts and fears, and to accept the challenge to cross the threshold, from my ordinary world into the *special world* of an American summer camp. During today's appointment, I say that I'm apprehensive about driving my new car because I don't want to have an accident. Sophie makes me realize that this is *hypothetical* worry, about something well into the future, and that they have no solution because the concern may not become a reality.

She then suggests that I get into the routine of classifying my doubts. When I have a worry, I have to first think about that worry, and if I determine it to be hypothetical, I need to try and remove it out of my head. The exception is a practical worry, which is a worry that I can do something about—for example, paying for a gas bill or getting to a meeting on time.

It's refreshing to realize that I'm dealing with something psychological, and that these stressful thoughts that I've been battling are the cause of the physical symptoms I've been experiencing. In removing these thoughts, I can avoid the trigger of stress. This can then eliminate symptoms of disorientation, low concentration and fatigue.

At the end of each telephone appointment, Sophie goes through a patient health questionnaire, known as a PHQ9, which is posted to me. I'm required to complete the questionnaire, prior to the appointments. Sophie uses the results of the questionnaire to review and support me with the therapy that I need. Each question I'm given follows a generic statement that is worded:

"Over the last two weeks, how often have you been bothered by any of the following problems?" The categories in question include:

- Having little interest in doing things,
- Feeling depressed and hopeless,
- Feeling tired or having little energy.

I'm required to answer every question with a number between zero and three. A zero means that the problem has no effect on me, and three indicates that the problem is a major one that affects me every day. I find myself answering most of the questions with a *one*, meaning that they occur in my thoughts occasionally.

The last question that Sophie always asks is:

"Have you had any thoughts of being better off dead, or of hurting yourself in some way?"

As always, I firmly reply with a "zero."

"So, just to reiterate, you don't have any thoughts of self-harm or suicide?" Sophie confirms.

"That's right," I reply.

I suppose if anyone were to answer that question with anything higher than a zero, then that person wouldn't benefit from simple telephone therapy. Cognitive behavioral therapy can be effective in dealing with stress, anxiety, and depression at the early stage, but what about those who have a prolonged mental health disorder? What about those who may suffer from hallucinations or who self-harm? It's not a *one size fits all* way of treatment. I think that more care and attention is absolute for those people. They need to conquer their negative thoughts by seeing practitioners on a regular basis, or by going to a rehabilitation centre with supervisory support.

I can already see benefits with the therapy that I'm getting, though, with greater control of my thoughts and behavior. I can focus on my future. This is the mentor's *magic* gift that I can use on my journey. It's been valuable to talk to someone about how I've been feeling—not just with Mum, but with a professional who has dealt with people suffering from anxiety, and who can understand my concerns and give me helpful advice.

17

STEADYING THE SHIP

I receive my passport back in the post and the American visa is displayed inside it. This is a special moment that confirms my legal entry to the U.S. next month.

Then an email pings in from Vince. It's directed to all international counselors who are now connected with Camp Ace Invaders. The email informs us that Vince has recently dealt with a newly instituted legal requirement from the American government. It requires background checks from all of his staff members.

Camp Ace Invaders belongs to the American Camp Association; therefore, they have to comply with the standards of practice, which are required from the summer camp industry. As a camp that works with children and an organization registered with the Pennsylvanian Department of State, it's now a requirement to comply with the nearly adjusted laws, particularly as they apply to employment protocols.

Irrespective of my DBS check, and never stepping foot in America, let alone Pennsylvania, I'm still required to obtain the following:

- A Pennsylvania criminal history record check through the Pennsylvania state police,
- A Pennsylvania child abuse history record check through the department of human services,
- An FBI clearance fingerprint-based national criminal history record check.

Copies of this paperwork will enable security for the reimbursement process, which will include my collection of earnings at camp. Therefore, the completion of these forms is now my highest priority.

A couple of days pass, and I'm not able to receive or find a certification form, regarding the child abuse history clearance, which I've completed. But with help from Chris at home and further guidance from Zoe, the criminal history record check eventually gets processed.

Nonetheless, I'm disgruntled by the continuous demands in this recruitment process. I've reached phases, thinking everything had been completed, but obstacles and expenses have continued to present themselves. It forces me to express my feelings to Bobby in an email.

Bobby replies later that day, and is apologetic about the harshness of the process and the fees involved in working at an international job. While Bobby empathizes with how daunting this process is for a newcomer like me, he reminds me that it wasn't just Camp Ace Invaders that recruited me to become a summer camp counselor. I've also used an agency to be proactive in pursuit of this job role. Bobby adds that if I'm deeply upset, then I should let the agency know, as it's their job to inform the international staff of the process for securing this position in the U.S.

Bobby mentions in his email that he's been impressed with me in the interviews, and that the camp is excited to have me on their staff list for the summer. But the last thing he wants is for a staff member to come into camp and work among the children with bitterness and resentment toward the recruitment process. Bobby apologizes in advance if he's off base in his rant, though he did correctly perceive my negativity in the email. His response is stern because he wants the camp to be a place for a fantastic experience, filled with nothing but positive vibes.

As extraordinary as technology is for communicating with people around the world, there are also inherent problems. One issue is that it can be difficult to interpret people's feelings from the context of their emails.

Regardless of this, I can clearly identify the emotion that Bobby is communicating when writing this email. Pure passion and respect from Bobby toward his beloved Camp Ace Invaders shines through in his words.

Regretting my previous email, I quickly reply to Bobby, letting him know that this whole process hasn't dampened my desire or excitement for the summer. I'll come to Camp Ace Invaders with no intention of having any negativity festering. I'm apologetic for coming across so negative in the last email, and the flight ticket nightmare hasn't helped my frustration. I also write how impressed I've been with Wild Packs for being such a helpful agency. Without them, I may never have found myself a summer camp.

After I hit the send button, I look away from the computer screen and through the window to a cloudy day. This matches my mood. I hope

I haven't elicited any problems at the camp from the negative tone of my previous email. I don't want this to taint their liking of me.

Bobby responds in the evening, relieved. He's glad that I'm still excited for camp and reiterates that the camp will be thrilled to have me. He assures me that if I have any further inquiries before my departure in mid-June, he's happy to help. I'm sure I'll email him with another inquiry soon.

18

FINAL PREPARATIONS

As the final weeks of preparation approach, I email Bobby again. This time I'm wondering what the arrangements should be for when I arrive at Scranton airport.

- Will it be okay to arrive at Camp Ace Invaders on that day?
- If not, what's the cheapest and easiest place to stay overnight?
- Will there be other international staff on the same flight as me?

Bobby replies promptly and answers my questions. He states that he can arrange a "pick-up vehicle" to collect me on the date I specified, even though it's two days early. Bobby also provides me with a phone number to use when I've landed in Scranton, to arrange a driver to pick me up, or to notify the camp if anything changes. He adds that it's possible for other staff members arriving on the same date and time as me. I just need to sit tight until other people's plans emerge. It's been valuable to have online interactions with a supportive individual, who has put my mind at ease during my final preparations.

The online staff handbook gives me added reassurance, which has a comprehensive list of what belongings I need to pack. On top of that, I've now involved myself into conversations on the Camp Ace Invader's staff page on Facebook, with one topic of debate being *what to pack,* which has come in very handy.

I'm careful about how much clothing I need at the summer camp. Even though I'll be wearing staff t-shirts most days, I'll also need clothing to last for the month of traveling after my employment finishes. I make sure that most of my clothing is labeled with my initials in permanent ink, to prevent losing anything while I'm living communally with others.

Despite the risk of damage or theft to expensive electronic items, which Camp Ace Invaders cannot be responsible for, I'll also be taking my laptop and phone. Strictly prohibited items at camp include drugs and alcohol, pocketknives, and guns (all for obvious reasons), including any type of toy gun. Poker chips are also prohibited to prevent the promotion of gambling to the kids. If these items are found and reported, it'll mean a confiscation until the end of the summer, or a firing, depending on the inappropriateness of the item.

Money and valuables are strongly suggested to be deposited into the main office with Zoe for our protection. I'm overruling this advice, however, and leaving my money and valuables in my suitcase inside the cabin. I'm not mentioning this to anyone and making sure that the suitcase is securely padlocked. That way, I'll avoid the risk of any complications when accessing my money when I need it.

During the last Monday appointment with Sophie from iTalk, I'm pleased to tell her that I'm feeling better about myself. I'm also excited about setting off to America next week. Since starting the counseling, I've had mail delivered to the house. The literature I've received has been useful in my therapy, for dealing with worry, and to prevent another psychological setback in the future. I've also been provided with a relaxation CD for meditation, which features peaceful sounds and a calmly spoken instructor. I haven't played it yet, but I appreciate the benefits that this method has on people.

All in all, I definitely made the right decision to use the telephone counseling. My physical symptoms have been greatly reduced, as has my irritability. Sophie has been advising me to write down my thoughts and feelings. For me, this isn't a case of *look at me and my life*, but more about getting things off my chest.

The counseling has also taught me how important it is for people to not bottle up any thoughts or feelings. I've learned about the harsh consequences, when psychological disorders go too far. This couldn't be made more evident than with the death of Robin Williams—a man who brought such joy and humor to our family through the television screen, especially with his appearance in *Mrs. Doubtfire*.

Sadly, the nature of Robin's death revealed that he didn't feel joyful and positive within himself. He didn't feel happy, regardless of the smiles on the outside. He reached an episode in his life that took him into a *danger zone*, which can lead to self-harm and suicide. Suicide is one of the biggest killers, especially in men under 50.

This shows that a large number of people with mental illnesses never seek help. I'm also becoming more aware of many people of today who don't get job satisfaction where they work, or who aren't in strong meaningful relationships. People may lack the self-confidence in achieving things they're aspiring to achieve, while others don't get that deep fulfillment in something they're currently focusing on.

A motivational speaker, whom I recently watched on a YouTube video, had directed his attention to people of my generation. The *millennials* as he has termed us. He explained that the reason people struggle to enjoy or succeed in life is because they can't rely on the instant gratification that they get on social media. The same instant gratification when they receive likes and comments on a photo they upload, or when they open their phone and see a message from a friend they wanted to talk to. This causes social media to become an addiction to people, which, in turn, leads to negative outcomes.

Using phones to message people who aren't there, especially during a job meeting or a family dinner, will cause dysfunctional relationships, social isolation (in reality), and your life will get worse. This is because life will become imbalanced, with more time spent using devices, and less time being unplugged and spending quality time with those who matter. So, what a lot of this boils down to is being able to find that balance and overcoming the obstacles of the digital world.

Another important aspect from this is being aware of yourself enough to identify when there's a problem and to do something about it. And I feel from my current experience that the best method of doing something about it is to talk it out with someone, albeit someone who listens and respects you.

I realize from my past that you can't suppress any negative remarks, insults, or stress, whether this occurs in school, within a sports team, at work, or in your social life. That isn't healthy. Instead, talking to people is important, and you don't even have to see them in person. You can just write to them or speak to them on the phone. It's that simple.

19

THE JOURNEY

The day that I leave England is a bright morning. I've laid out what clothes I'm wearing for the day. My rucksack and suitcase welcomes me outside the bedroom door. Once I'm ready to leave, Mum, being the cautious person that she is, does a thorough check around the house to make sure I don't leave anything important behind. Dad insists on carrying my suitcase, and places it into the trunk of the car before sitting in the driver's seat with Chris in the back.

I kiss goodbye to Rosie the cat, and we then set off in the car. I'm feeling content and listen to mainstream rock bands on my iPod, which includes songs from the Red Hot Chili Peppers, Foo Fighters, Linkin Park, and Queens of the Stone Age. This maintains the positivity I'm currently feeling.

When we arrive at Heathrow airport, I take the necessary steps. I check in at the airline desk with my e-ticket and passport, and thankfully my luggage is not exceeding the weight limit to board the flight. Then we move up the escalator to the next floor where I'll be greeted with further security checks. But before that, we have a hot drink and a Danish pastry in the café for breakfast.

To our amazement, on the way to the café, we brush past England football legend, John Barnes. He's still easily recognizable. I'm not sure why it came as a surprise to see John Barnes, since celebrities need to use the airlines just like us. That is, unless they have a private jet, of course!

It soon became time for the security checks to commence. Just before I pass the doors, I turn to my family.

"Look after yourself, George, and enjoy it," says Dad.

"Have a great time, mate," says Chris.

"Remember to keep in touch with us on Skype whenever you get the time," Mum adds as we exchanged hugs with each other.

I wave goodbye before approaching the next room. There is the moment of doubt, right before I cross the threshold, away from the ordinary world. I know I'm taking a gamble, because until I've absorbed this whole experience, there'll always be a fraction of doubt, that something might go wrong or that I might not enjoy it. I've been connected with Bobby and Vince so regularly in the last couple of months. But will my perceptions of them from the technological world of social media be dimmed when we finally meet? Surely, I'm not alone in finding the anticipation of this experience daunting, as well as exciting? I need to remain confident in myself and internalize the importance of keeping my composure when I'm out of my comfort zone.

I walk along a corridor until I get to the process controlled by conveyor belts, x-ray screens, and metal detecting machines. I think about the minor purpose that the human workers have in this section of the airport, compared to the robots that are screening my belongings.

I have no illegal possessions to declare and I go through this zone without being flagged by the metal detection devices. Then, after waiting at the gate for my flight and boarding my seat on the American Airline's aircraft, I take my last few glimpses at English soil for the next few months. I'm about to endure an eight-hour flight, which will be the longest journey I've experienced in the air.

I sit beside a middle-aged woman of the obese variety, and as I turn my head to the left of me I see three spare seats in the next aisle. I wait an hour in case someone may snatch them, and then finally transfer myself over to the space of better legroom, comfort, and the greater likelihood of sleeping longer. I'm relieved to move away from that woman, who's snoring in her deep sleep, like a grizzly bear in hibernation.

Later in the flight, I take advantage of the complimentary food and drink. I would be lying if I said I was looking forward to airplane food, although the microwavable pizza pocket and the melt-in-your-mouth chocolate fudge cake are tasty enough for me. There's also a television screen, a hi-tech commodity, built into the back of every seat. The screen that's facing me has one channel dedicated to the journey of the flight and where we're currently positioned on the map, with the correct time zone and climate. There's also a page on the touchscreen that shows an option of movies that you can play and watch at any time. I try to start watching the film *Step Brothers*, which will feature one of my favorite comedians, Will Ferrell, who'll help ease my recent tension. As I press play, I realize my headphones are too short for me to comfortably slouch back in my chair to watch the film. Complications with electronic devices aren't a new thing to me. New devices like the recent smartphones can be too smart for their own good, and I only use a small percentage of the apps on offer.

I give up on watching a movie during the flight and decided to get some sleep, with the help of my neck pillow that I quickly inflate. It doesn't seem long until I'm awakened by the sun shining through the windows on my right, as we approach the final part of the flight. We're now in the afternoon hours of northeast Pennsylvania.

As the tires hit the tarmac in a steady landing, I hear a ripple of applause from many of the commuters, showing their appreciation to the pilots for a successful flight. I'm now in Scranton airport, and eagerly anticipating the arrival of a minibus associated with Camp Ace Invaders, which I have organized with Bobby previously on email. When I set foot off the airplane, the air has a warmer feel to it, compared to England.

Then as I walk into the airport and wait to collect my luggage, I see a woman who looks familiar. It dawns on me that she's a specialist counselor that I remember seeing on the Facebook group for Camp Ace Invaders staff. We smile at each other, as our eyes meet, and we start talking. She reveals to me that her name is Amanda. She'll be an arts and crafts specialist at the summer camp. She also informs me that she just made the call to arrange a driver to pick her up, also as recommended to her by Bobby. This takes the pressure off me in arranging the final phase of transport.

We eventually see the minibus with the summer camp's emblem printed on the side and walk toward it. Out jumps a muscular man with long, frizzy hair that dangles down from his baseball cap.

"Hey guys, are you hitching a ride with me to Camp Ace Invaders?" the man asks in his strong American accent.

When we confirm that we need a lift, I hop onto the minibus and am welcomed by two other women who'll also be working at the summer camp. They've been picked up from the airport in New York, which is approximately an hour and a half away from camp, by vehicle.

The man then springs into the driver's seat.

"So, my name's Brad, guys, but you can call me Beefy."

We exchange questions with each other and it turns out that the three women are also from the UK. Two of them have worked previously at Camp Ace Invaders and cannot wait to resume the experience once again. The pleasant mood from the group energizes me after the long flight, and I'm feeling excited to commence my first experience at the summer camp.

20

FIRST IMPRESSIONS

"Would you like to stop off at Walmart to get some grub before we head back to camp?" asked Beefy.

We all agreed to this, and Beefy informed us Brits of the humongous size of the Walmart supermarket, and told us that we'll be spoilt for choice on what we want to buy. As I enter through the doors of Walmart, Beefy's description of the place lives up to my expectations.

I see sights that I've never encountered before—giant marshmallows in buckets, barrels of corn snacks, boxes of Pop-Tarts and 5kg jars of Nutella and peanut butter. Every brand of cereal, biscuit, chocolate, candy, ice-cream, potato chips and soft drink are all on offer here. I'm stuck between amazement and bewilderment—the same feeling that one would assume the children experienced in the story of *Charlie and the Chocolate Factory.* There's also a Subway joint inside the supermarket, and I decide to just have a foot-long turkey and ham sub. All other options in the supermarket make me indecisive.

On the final journey to the campsite, I take a gander out of the window of the minibus. I notice how different the scenery looks here. There are various altitudes of land and I can see forests stretching for miles. The sweet aroma of pine is intoxicating when we drive closely through the woodlands.

The roads appear unsafe, with the surface rising and falling by the slopes, similar to what's experienced on a roller coaster. Both sides of the road are cut off by cliff edges and we're elevated to a considerable height. I dread to think how many fatalities there must've been from reckless driving. With that thought, Beefy talks to the group on a serious note:

"You need to be careful driving late at night over here, guys—you never know when the wild deer might scatter onto the road, and they have no perception of you and your vehicle. In addition to damaging your vehicle, you can get into serious trouble for killing a deer."

"What kind of trouble?" asks Amanda.

"Well, you can lose your license if the authorities hear about it, especially if it's a white-tailed deer, since their population is threatened by many predators. If this occurs while you are under the influence of alcohol and the police find out, then you'll have a prison sentence for sure," Beefy explains.

Understandably, the state of Pennsylvania, as well as the summer camp, takes drunk and disorderly behavior very seriously. And even though I wouldn't be driving under the influence of alcohol, I'm still reluctant to the idea of driving in this area as it involves a greater deal of risk due to the environment and wildlife. I wouldn't want to be held responsible for a damaged vehicle belonging to the camp.

Besides that point, the vehicle policy states that every staff member is responsible for arranging their own transportation on days off. And no vehicles are available to staff on any of the nights off. When I first read this I remember thinking how difficult it could be to arrange a lift to The Chasers bar.

We arrive through the welcoming gate, which features the words "Camp Ace Invaders." After the minibus is parked, we followed Beefy to the headquarters building. Arriving at camp feels strange to me because I really have no idea what I'm getting myself into.

After I get out of the minibus, I'm greeted by several of the head counselors. I'm too overwhelmed to remember all their names, but I shake hands with Tigger, who's going to be a group leader of the Middy division, which is the same age group of campers I'll be supervising. I'm also greeted by Bobby, the camp's associate director and the man that I've regularly communicated with through email. I distinctively recognize Bobby's appearance from that interview I had with him.

"Hello, George; it's really great to see you."

"Good to see you too, Bobby. I had a smooth journey over. Thanks for supporting me in my preparations."

"That's great you made it safely over, and you're very welcome."

Weirdly enough, seeing a total stranger's excitement at me arriving safely at the camp was very uplifting for me. All the tension that I experienced on the way up has disappeared for a brief moment.

Minutes later, Tigger offers to show me the bunkhouse that I'll be living in for the next couple of months. He walks over to a two-seater vehicle that resembles a golf cart. Tigger walks with a certain swagger and wears a snapback and long basketball shorts. This appearance establishes a free-spirited person. He strikes me as a popular character here, and a leader.

Tigger drives me over in the cart with my luggage on the back and drops me off at my bunkhouse for the summer. It's a large wooden cabin. As I walk into the bunkhouse, I see that all the bunkbeds are unprepared, with just foam mattresses on each one. There are four top bunkbeds, which Tigger tells me are for the counselors. He brings in bed sheets, a duvet, and a pillow into my room. It's totally bare inside the bunkhouse, as I put away my luggage onto the empty shelves. The next task I have is to make my bed for the night. This is a task that I'll be urging all my campers to do soon, too.

During the first night, I met Gavin, an English guy with blond, spiky hair. He's from Essex. It comes as a pleasant surprise that he has a keen interest in football, and that he's a Spurs supporter, too. There's a small group of us sitting on the swings, and each of us are looking directly at the light of the sunset reflecting off the Maple Lagoon waterfront. There's a fresh earthy fragrance that whiffs toward us in the gentle breeze. We chat, and, in our pauses, we listen to the soft inland murmurs until the darkness gradually draws in. This is a beautiful view that I can easily get used to.

It's a surreal experience as I prepare to sleep in an empty wooden bunkhouse. I'm hoping to have a good night's sleep after the tiring journey over from England. I finally fall asleep. And then BANG! The door of the bunkhouse slams open, and I feel my heart beating a little faster. A bright light flashes over me and I turn my head to see a bulky man with a bald head. I'm worried in case it's Vince, the camp's director.

"George, is that you?"

"Err...yes, it is," I reply, feeling confused.

"I'm Martin, one of the head counselors. You forgot to sign yourself in tonight," he chuckled back.

"Oh yeah, sorry about that," I say, feeling embarrassed.

"It's important you sign in every night, dude, so that we know you're safe for the night. Three strikes for not doing this and you'll get an off-duty taken away. Have a good sleep."

This is something I really need to come to terms with, as I don't fancy being awakened so abruptly again this summer.

21

THE SETTLING

The second day is gloomy at Camp Ace Invaders, with overcast skies and a strong breeze. It's very un-American weather, based on my preconceived notions. Those of us who have already migrated to the camp are now awaiting the crowds of counselors and campers that are yet to come. But for now, we've been sent around the campsite doing errands in preparation for the summer activities. I've been assigned the less than joyous task of helping to construct the stage in the sports hall, which will be used for spokespeople to host meetings of importance. It'll also be used by all the performers and entertainers during the evening shows.

Once the morning errands are complete, I manage to make a new friend. His name is Blake, and he's of similar height to me, but with a broader physique and naturally tanned skin. He's from Los Angeles and he's going to start studying at university after camp. Blake is using these two months to pick up money—not for educational resources, like textbooks, but to spend on the social expenses, such as booze and the hiring of frat parties. I'm sure his parents aren't aware of his intentions.

In the afternoon we both return to our bunkhouses, along with Gavin, to quickly change into sportswear and lace our boots to play some *soccer* between the goals that have already had the nets fitted to them. We manage to borrow a football from one of the senior soccer specialists. We enjoy our first activity of the summer, taking it in turns at being the strikers and taking shots, while the other one being the goalkeeper between the sticks. This takes me back to some of my fondest memories that brought me and my brothers closer together—when we played football at the park in our hometown. There are no goals in this park and no proper pitch. But with our ball and two trees 10 yards apart, playing there has always made us happy. Today we played on the soccer field until it was suppertime.

Darkness then falls on another day at camp. It feels bizarre as I sit alone on the bed after signing myself in for the night. There's the sharp fragrance of sawn wood, which obviously comes from the wooden infrastructure of the bunkhouse. It's the complete opposite of a cozy and luxurious place to live.

This feeling decreases the next day, somewhat, when the next two counselors arrive at the bunkhouse, escorted on a cart by a head counselor, the same as I was. One of them is Brett, a guy from Ohio, who's going to be a specialist in Field Hockey. The other is Nate, a guy taller than me who lives locally in Pennsylvania. He's going to be a basketball specialist.

After introducing myself, I decide to check out the facilities at the counselors' lounge and make my first Skype call. I have free access to the computers, Wi-Fi, and two telephones. I use my Google Chromebook for Skype because the camp's computers don't have built-in webcams. I was informed on my first day here that the Wi-Fi is fairly weak, even at the best of times, and my laptop isn't the most suitable device for Skype calls. But after organizing a time with Chris on Facebook, I manage to connect with him, Mum, and Dad. The call lasts approximately half an hour. The conversation is occasionally disrupted due to the poor reception within the wilderness of northeast Pennsylvania.

Besides that, this conversation in the counselors' lounge puts into perspective how astonishing the invention of Skype really is—that you're able to see and chat with family and friends in any country. In the years since I was born, the development of technology has seen a vast increase. It really is intriguing in an impressive way.

22

ORIENTATION WEEK – PART 1

Saturday soon arrives, and camp is a lot busier and more exciting, with all the counselors arriving. The cabins have a more homely feel about them, and increased activity is happening across all the sports facilities. There are footballs flying off the soccer pitches. You can hear a collection of basketballs bouncing inside the sports hall, and the hoops of the outdoor basketball courts are forever occupied. Counselors are continuously playing singles and doubles matches on the three outdoor tennis courts. And as I look onto the greenery, beside the circus pavilion, I see two instructors, in their leotards, swinging together in the sky, in harmony. They're practicing their skills for their flying trapeze routines.

People are making friends fast and the laughter and chatter can be heard throughout. Robert, the forth counselor of Bunkhouse G has also arrived just before lunchtime. He's a Yorkshire lad who's easily recognizable by his accent. He's going to be a general counselor, just like me. Shortly after lunch, the bugle sounds, and then a loud voice projects out of the speakers.

"Can everyone please come over to the outdoor basketball court next to the sports hall for the first icebreaker! I repeat—please now come to the first icebreaker outside the sports hall!"

Within minutes, everyone is huddled together. Facing all of us is a row of head counselors, elevated on the sports hall balcony. It feels like I'm one of the contestants in *The Hunger Games*, eagerly waiting to hear who is nominated for the upcoming battle. Vince, the camp's owner and director, steps forward.

"Greetings, counselors. We welcome you all to Camp Ace Invaders. We're happy to see you, and we hope you enjoy your summer with us!"

I feel delighted, and Vince's welcome speech is met with a round of applause with shrill whistling. Vince's wife, Marie, then continues the announcement.

"Welcome to your first icebreaker. Today we will keep it simple with an old favorite that we can all remember from childhood. Rock, paper, scissors! Each game you play will be determined by the best of three goes. If you win a match, you stay on the court until you lose. The losers will stand on the edge of the court cheering whoever has beaten them or their opponents. May the best man or woman win!"

The announcement reverberates inside us and hands fly in the air during an almighty cheer. My first game of rock, paper, scissors is against Greg, whom I've only just met. He appears to be of East Asian origin and is the only staff member to have a blue bandana tied around his forehead.

On the first go, I succeed with paper beating rock. On the second go, Greg wins with rock beating scissors. The third game, I win and clinch the match with rock beating scissors again. My luck runs out in the second match, when I lose to Amy—an attractive looking lady, who has the look of a cheerleader, with a white crop top and a pink, frilly skirt.

All that's missing is her holding two large pom-poms. I cheer her on for the next contest.

As the icebreaker progresses, each player still in the competition develops extensive support, until the entire workforce of counselors is divided into two, supporting their respective players for the final contest. To my surprise, Beefy is the eventual winner, and a melee of people surrounds him in jubilation. Amongst the cheering, I see Fredric, who I met at the embassy. I make a mental note to catch up with him sometime. Beefy is overjoyed at his win and is lifted up into the air by a group of counselors. He reminds me of a pop superstar crowd surfing above his fans.

Icebreakers occur regularly during the first four days of orientation week. The key objective of these games is to get everyone familiar with each other, and to make new friends. The next icebreaker is based on the sitcom, *How I Met Your Mother*, though I don't understand the meaning behind this as it's something I've never watched. Two-thirds of the workforce is in pairs and linking arms. They wander around the basketball court until one person in the pair finds someone standing on their own that they know, but who the other person in the pair doesn't know. That counselor in the pair then has to introduce their partner to the other person.

"Hey, Rachel. Have you met my friend, Matt?" I say on this particular occasion.

Then Rachel and Matt begin talking about themselves for a minute or two. They then link arms and find someone else, while I wait to be greeted by another couple of counselors. The game continues in the same way for roughly 10 minutes.

There's also an icebreaker called "Flippy Cup," where all the counselors are divided into groups of 15. Each game consists of two teams of 15 standing on opposite sides of a table, facing one another. The table has two lines of disposable plastic cups, each one filled with water (though traditionally it's an alcoholic beverage). There's one cup for every team member. At one end of the table, the first member of each team starts the game off by drinking the entirety of their water as quickly as possible. Then they place their empty cup on the edge of the table, open side up. They proceed to flip their cup until it lands face down on the table. When a team member correctly lands their cup on the table, the next person in their team goes, and so on, until a whole team has successfully flipped all their cups. The winners are the team that does this the fastest and this tournament keeps everyone well hydrated for the day ahead.

Another icebreaker requires all of the counselors to split into small groups again. Each of the people within a group has to think of a food with the same first letter as their first name. Then each person reveals their food to the group and, with each turn, the list of food gets longer. It becomes increasingly difficult to memorize what everyone has brought to the *imaginary picnic*.

"Eddie brought eggs, Robert brought roast potatoes, Charlotte brought chocolate, Brian brought bagels, Megan, ...uhh."

I hesitantly answer the group's picnic until I can no longer remember. Some counselors are surprisingly good at this game, and effortlessly complete their group's picnic in front of the watching eyes of the entire workforce.

The following icebreaker requires all the counselors to split up into small groups again. In each group, they all have to make noises that resemble the same species of animals. All the groups are then mixed together with everyone else inside the sports hall, and we have to try to find each of our group members by signaling the animal noises that we performed before, while also demonstrating the actions of the animal that makes the noise.

"Oh. Oh. Ahh! Ahh!"

I screech like a chimpanzee as I bend my hands into my armpits and stagger around trying to find my group among the elephants, lions, and horses in the sports hall.

There's also an icebreaker that involves a watermelon. We split into groups of 20 across the three tennis courts, and within each group, a watermelon is perched on a sports cone. Four members of each group then have to put goggles on and sit on chairs, surrounding the fruit. Each of the four people has to stretch a bunch of elastic bands around the middle area of the watermelon. A head counselor keeps track of how many elastic bands are stretched around it throughout the game. Once enough elastic bands have been pulled onto the watermelon, each of the four people is given a question that they have to answer before leaving the watermelon. At each of the group's station, there's a head counselor dishing out the questions. Most questions are obscure and randomly funny.

"Would you rather have legs as fingers or fingers as legs, and why?" was one question that received a lot of laughs.

"Would you rather fall into a pool of skittles or a pool of marshmallows, and why?" was another question.

Once everyone has answered the question, another four sit down on the seats, fearing the worst. These next four people have to stretch a bunch more elastic bands around the squeezed watermelon and answer a new set of questions. The game ends when the watermelon explodes all over the four people nearest to the fruit, due to the pressure from the elastic bands, which is why we all wear clothes that we don't mind getting stained.

The games take longer than expected to finish. The watermelons turn out to be very robust and withstand a lot of pressure from the elastic bands. I'll never forget when Bobby joins a group, whose watermelon is nearing its end. It looks somewhat like a cashew nut by this point. Bobby stays sitting in one of the four chairs for the remainder of the game, until the watermelon explodes, which happens in comical fashion.

"No. No. NOOO!"

Bobby is helpless and encircled by laughter as the tip of the watermelon slowly tilts downwards, in his direction. It looks human controlled, like the machine gun ammunition of an army tank, aiming itself perfectly at Bobby.

Then, all of a sudden, a blast of watermelon juice sprays Bobby's face. He couldn't have positioned his chair any better. As Bobby wipes the lenses of his glasses in sheer amazement, all of the counselors are left in stitches.

One of the final icebreakers involves each counselor being given a slip of paper to write the name of a famous person or fictional character, and then sticking the paper on another person's forehead. Each of us frantically questions other people, looking for clues about who we are. Basically, its charades galore taking place inside the sports hall. The game ends when a counselor correctly guesses the name on their forehead, or if they simply give up. I happened to be the Michelin Man at one point, but couldn't guess this white, blubbery mascot correctly.

23

ORIENTATION WEEK – PART 2

Midway through orientation week, there's another announcement for all counselors to report to the sports hall. We're all welcomed by Vince and Marie when we arrive and are told to be seated on the benches. Vince then reveals some shocking stories that have happened to former members at Camp Ace Invaders.

The first thing brought to our attention is the existence of a very pleasant bar called The Chasers. It's a couple of miles away from the summer camp, and we can use it whenever we have an evening free to ourselves when we're off-duty. He then reminds us of how important it is to drink responsibly, because when we come back to the cabins and the kids are feeling homesick, we have to act as professionals. We can't act in a drunk and disorderly way or smell of booze. This is a violation of the rules at Camp Ace Invaders and will result in an instant dismissal—we'd have to leave that night. Our departure won't wait until the next morning.

I remember reading in the staff manual about how a termination will be immediate for someone after a confirmed firing. The fired staff member will be taken back to their bunkhouse by a head staff member, who'll remain with that person until they're removed from the premises.

That head staff member will oversee the packing of the former staff member's belongings, and this will take place at an appropriate time that doesn't interfere with any of the campers' daily activities.

If requested, the former staff member will receive a cash advance of up to five percent of their remaining base salary. The rest of their salary will be processed with payroll at the end of the summer and will be mailed to their address on file with their personal items. If a staff member, in this predicament, has their own car on campus, then that car will need to be loaded up with their belongings, and the person will have to leave in their car immediately. Or if they require transportation, then this will be provided for them at the convenience of the camp. They'll be asked if they prefer to be taken to the Scranton bus terminal or airport, or a local hotel of their choosing, depending on the time of the termination, and they'll need to arrange their next accommodation themselves.

I focus again on Vince. He announces that five years ago he proudly welcomed four Irishmen to Camp Ace Invaders. They had incredible personalities, and their friendly nature made them very popular characters at the summer camp. But one night the four Irishmen decided to go for drinks at The Chasers in a hired car. They ended up drinking excessive amounts of alcohol, and ultimately, one of them was drunk driving on the way back to the summer camp. They ended up crashing into another car and killing the other driver and their passenger. The Irishmen survived the incident, yet it put them all behind bars for drunk driving and manslaughter. Vince believes that they still have another five years left in prison.

This really startles me. I'm fully aware of the effects of drinking excessively, but many of these counselors are a couple of years younger than me, maybe more. They may not be aware of their limits yet. I'm looking forward to drinking a cool, refreshing pint of beer after a hard day's work. It'll be a great opportunity to make friends. But Vince's speech comes with a powerful dose of reality. We have to be disciplined while we work at Camp Ace Invaders, and we have to remember that we're here to make the experience wonderful for the children. It's not a holiday for us, as we're employees of the summer camp.

Another catastrophic story occurred at the summer camp in 1985. A young girl was standing too close to a fellow camper during a golf lesson and was struck in the throat by the other child's backswing of the golf club. As a result, she tragically died on the way to hospital. This isn't only an important message to us counselors about keeping ourselves safe during activities, but to also pay close attention to the children we're supervising. We must take their safety into consideration, especially during their activity sessions.

"We don't want to be the ones having to confess the death of a loved one over the phone to the child's distraught parents... Not again."

Goosebumps rise on my arms and the hairs on my neck stand on end. Vince speaks meaningfully, and his eyes well up. His face, unlike a mask, has every emotion written on it.

The third disastrous incident that's brought to our attention is that of an adventure specialist. Some of the adventure specialists partake in leading the high-rope activities, based within the woodlands of the campground. This particular adventure specialist had invited two of her colleagues into the woods one evening when it was dark and wet. She demonstrated the tree climbing skills that she had recently mastered, without the safety equipment in place. But suddenly, she fell from a considerable height. She broke one of her legs and had multiple spinal and pelvic fractures from the impact of the landing. Even though Vince and the head counselors were saddened to learn about the severity of the injury that the specialist counselor sustained, she was instantly fired for her actions, before being escorted to the hospital.

The other two counselors who accompanied the adventure specialist into the woods were also fired. They had violated their professional contracts, because they were on-duty staff and were required to be stationed with their children by the cabins, or with their campers in the sports hall, if they're in attendance for the evening show. No one, apart from off-duty staff, should leave the camp boundaries after dark.

The following day of orientation week is a "free day," and I spend the afternoon with Blake, along with Megan, who I've recently become friendly with, and many other colleagues. We decide to travel in several cars to a place that's 45 minutes away to do cliff diving. I'm skeptical of this specific activity because it doesn't sound particularly safe. But some of the experienced counselors have been raving about how fun this activity will be.

As soon as we park, I instantly get an uncomfortable feeling that this is a bad idea. As we walk past the parking lot, we're warned by signs that say, "no diving" and "no litter on the premises." Yet most of us are wearing swimwear in anticipation of going diving. Blake and I bring a crate of Budweiser beer along, which I bought from an off-license shop, before Megan drove us to the destination.

We stroll out of the parking lot and along a downhill trail within a woodland, and within minutes I see the picturesque setting for the cliff diving. A waterfall and small streams surround us, as do giant rocks and boulders. Cliff drops are around 20 feet from where we perch ourselves to sunbathe.

It doesn't take long before the first counselors demonstrate their bravery by plunging headlong into water. The male colleagues are probably doing this to impress their crushes. I'm content to get a tan on the rocks while drinking a beer. I wince at the risky dives that some of the counselors perform in quick successions, especially the backflips, which they seem to have mastered in previous water-based activities.

One specific drop of approximately 50 feet can be clearly seen from where I'm sitting. Harvey is one of the speedboat specialists and decides to perform an epic plummet off the ledge. It impresses everyone, including me. I take footage of this breathtaking dive on my phone camera.

Eventually, the evening arrives and the sun begins to set. An hour later, I'm glad to be chilling in my cabin, having witnessed no accidents.

24

ORIENTATION WEEK – PART 3

The next day, I move into another watery environment. There's swimming tests today, run by the supervisors of the swimming pool. It's important to pass the swimming tests in order to demonstrate to the camp that we're capable of supervising our campers at the Maple Lagoon waterfront. And in the worst-case scenario, we can help save a camper from drowning, even though everyone must wear lifejackets. The tests consist of swimming 10 lengths of the swimming pool in under 20 minutes, and treading water for a further two minutes. I manage to swim the lengths fine, though I'm very tired afterward.

I always find swimming tiring. Maybe I have a poor technique, using extra effort unnecessarily to move across the water. When it comes to the treading water part, I find it almost unbearable. After one minute of doing this, my head keeps sinking halfway into the water. I'm pumping my legs and flapping my arms to keep my head bobbing above the surface. In desperation, I grip onto the wall of the swimming pool with my left hand when the supervisors aren't looking, just to maintain my position on the surface.

Finally, and to my relief, the test is over. I'm extremely tired. It then takes me a good 30 minutes to recuperate in the bunkhouse as I return to a normal breathing pattern.

The same day, we also have to transfer every camper's luggage to the right cabins. The luggage arrives after lunch. Numerous trucks enter and are filled with the biggest pile of duffle bags I've ever seen. Some of these duffle bags are enormous in size, to say the least. I realize that it's going to be a physically demanding and lengthy task to carry each bag to its allocated cabin, which is indicated either on a tag or on the material of the bags in thick, black marker pen.

This task requires a joint effort from every single member of staff, which Vince clarifies to us in his announcement, prior to the mission. It's advised that counselors carry the luggage in pairs. It's advice that I follow, yet there are brawny male counselors who carry the bags on their own. I guess that their machismo is a way of impressing the lady counselors.

This task is to be carried out over two full days, and many of us grow tired during the first day. The more duffle bags that are transported, the more I can hear deep breathing from colleagues that I brush past. I cannot help but notice the patches of sweat spreading on the shirts of the counselors, or their strikingly red faces.

The second day of this mammoth task requires several water breaks in between mealtimes, with exhausted counselors slumped on benches and steps of the bunkhouses, trying to gather extra energy and hydration. The duffle bags seem to grow heavier as the day passes. I'm beginning to wonder whether the campers themselves are actually trapped inside the bags, along with their luggage. At this moment, I reflect on my dad and how he's had to use self-determination throughout his life, doing heavy manual work to survive. To sum up Dad's philosophy, "You have to keep going until the job is done."

This day is humid and overcast, and it ends up raining in the afternoon, very heavily at times. We're still required to persevere through this treacherous weather, wearing anything we have that's waterproof. This day involves pep talks from senior members, and songs chanted in our groups to energize us, create a positive mood, and avoid the feeling of giving up and surrendering. Now I realize the effectiveness of the icebreakers from the first few days. They helped to generate a bond between everyone in the workforce, and having this camaraderie at camp, facilitates a more productive and cooperative approach to this strenuous activity.

By 4 p.m. on Friday, the second day of moving the oversized duffle bags, we're down to one last truck. Whether people have pulled their weight in completing this task, or not, we're all relieved to be seeing the last of them.

"Woooo. Yeah! Let's go, Camp Ace Invaders!" I hear a group of women screaming in the distance as the stack dwindles down to just a handful of duffle bags remaining. Motivational chanting breaks out.

"A to the C to the E to the I to the N to the V to the A to the D to the E to the R to S! What does that spell? Camp Ace Invaders!"

The atmosphere at camp has become very spirited, and a huge cheer breaks out when the last set of luggage enters the bunkhouses. The day ends with a refreshing pitcher of beer at The Chasers once I hitch a ride to the bar. Following this, we still have to remember to sign ourselves into the camp before midnight, which can be difficult once you're tipsy.

The weekend consists of unpacking a shedload of luggage belonging to the campers. A head counselor, named Randy, demonstrates how we're supposed to fold the clothes, and how they should be stacked in each of the cubby shelves. We're also shown where the other items are stored inside the bunkhouse, such as towels, footwear, and cosmetics. I quickly realize that this is going to be a prolonged and tedious activity that we'll need to complete by the end of the weekend. The bags seem to take forever to empty.

To help us along the way, Nate switched on his speakers and iPod, and we listen to his music. It's mainly a mix between rock 'n' roll and country music. Robert and Brett work on the campers' luggage on one side of the room, while Nate and I cooperate on the other side. It doesn't take a rocket scientist to recognize that all the kids have taken too much clothing with them, all of which has been crammed inside their duffle bags. Some contain tightly sealed polythene bags that are unnecessarily vacuum packed.

Another quick realization is that the bunkhouses aren't blessed with much storage space. It's a difficult chore—to place all the clothing into the cubbies, which are now labeled with the names of the campers, so they can distinguish where their belongings are. After a few hours, the bunkhouse is definitely showing a lot more character. It's become homey, compared to how bare I remember it looking on my first night.

Having said that, the bunkhouse looks more like a sports store, rather than a place to live. All the floor mats and bed sheets are branded with emblems of famous American football or basketball teams, and half of the clothing stored in the cubbies also features famous sports teams from across the United States.

On Sunday afternoon, our bunkhouse is inspected by head counselor, Calvin. We find ourselves criticized for a couple of errors, including a couple of t-shirts that weren't *perfectly* folded. But these are minor errors that we quickly manage to correct during Calvin's inspection. We feel relieved to complete this next task on the camp's brutal agenda, but we don't feel ready to face the campers just yet.

25

THE FIRST ARRIVALS

When Monday comes, I put on one of my eight staff tops that are to be worn daily from now on. Each counselor has three white and three red t-shirts, one long-sleeve gray shirt (for those cooler days), and a black vest top (for those hotter days). They all display the year and the camp's logo on the front, with the word *STAFF* printed in bold letters on the back. This will enable visitors to know who we are, as well as the public for offsite trips. The children all have their own t-shirts in red and yellow, which we've organized into their cubbies for them.

Bobby has informed me and the three other counselors in my bunkhouse that our first two campers are set to arrive today. We all work together to make a colorful banner out of felt-tip pens belonging to the arts and crafts center. This is for Stan and Josh.

Over the course of the day, the campers arrive by the hundreds. It then gets to roughly 3 p.m. when we see a bus driving in. This bus holds campers from the Middy division. The four of us walk over to the entrance of the camp with our banner. Suddenly, the heavens break open and rain starts pouring. Robert and I raise the banner among the cluster of other counselors who are also waiting to meet their new campers for the first time. Our banners begin to soften in the rain, and the ink starts rolling down the paper.

"Bunkhouse G, over here!"

We call this out to enlighten Stan and Josh that we'll be their new counselors. We've been told that the campers will already know their bunkhouse assignments.

All of a sudden, two boys break through the crowd of 10- to 11-year-olds. They come running over to us, full of excitement. Bunkhouse G then rejoices and I give Stan and Josh high fives. We unite as one team.

The bed areas are presented to Stan and Josh as they walk into the cabin. Josh says how cool the interior of the cabin looks, which shows that all the effort in the last few days has paid off. Josh then retrieves an indoor basketball from his bag and starts bouncing the ball around the room. He and Stan practice taking shots at an indoor basketball hoop that's attached to the inner side of the front door.

It's a surreal moment—seeing these boys bond so quickly, having been apart for a whole year. This demonstrates how strong the friendships are that develop at Camp Ace Invaders. No length of time apart can weaken the connections that are made. A few moments later, we hear the bugle for supper.

"Oh boy, I'm hungry. I wonder what's for supper. I hope it's burgers!" Stan says in his high-pitched voice.

In my head, I start to compare Stan to Ralph Wiggum from *The Simpsons*. This comparison is due to the tone of his voice and his appearance.

Supper has no burgers, but it does include the ever-popular tacos with a mixture of mincemeat, mixed veg, nacho cheese, and other sauces, including guacamole. Stan indulges in a plateful of food to satisfy his hunger. Stan and Josh are then happy to discover that cookies and ice-cream are on the menu for dessert. Supper finishes in a joyful manner, with the latest pop music playing throughout the dining hall, including the song "Uptown Funk" by Bruno Mars. This galvanizes many of the campers to stand on their benches and dance along to the tunes.

The next day sees the arrival of the rest of the campers. The buses are scheduled to arrive at the camp from 2 p.m. onwards. Robert and I decide to meet the first set of campers who arrive, while Nate and Brett are situated in the bunkhouse to supervise Stan and Josh. We alternate our responsibilities with every bus arrival. The number of campers grows and grows until there are 10 campers in the bunkhouse.

26

THE TYPICAL LIFESTYLE

Our cabin's previously serene atmosphere develops into noisy chaos in a matter of hours on the first evening with all the campers. Mini-basketballs catapult from one side of the room to the other. Other campers are jumping on their beds and playing with flashlights and Rubik's cubes. I don't know how to react within this disorderly mess, and it doesn't help not knowing many names.

"Okay. Everyone, just calm down; it's getting too noisy in here!" shouts Robert. This has minimal effect.

"We've got to get used to this, mate," I say to Robert with a chuckle.

A week goes by, and we've all adapted to the summer camp's daily structure. The bugle goes off, ringing in our ears at 7:30 a.m. to get us out of bed. The bugle sounds again at 8 a.m. and our bunkhouse walks to the dining hall for breakfast, still half asleep.

At 8:45 a.m. the bugle then goes off for the morning line-up. The line-up consists of Bobby informing us about any updates on the campground and the upcoming fixtures for the sports teams of each division, which compete against other summer camps in the local area. This ends with a pledge of allegiance to the U.S. flag.

After line-up, we all return to our bunkhouses for morning clean-up which involves making the beds and tidying the bunkhouse fo inspection. A head counselor enters 30 minutes later and checks the cleanliness of the cabin. The head counselor's assessment goes toward the "cleanest bunkhouse of the week" award, which can result in a movie night in the camp's 70 seater theatre room or a bunkhouse party, with pizza or cookies.

Then there's the first activity and the second activity, which Bunkhouse G do together, followed by the first elective, which is an activity that campers have chosen as their most favorite to partake in. After that is a call for lunch, then there's a rest-hour at the bunkhouses, which gives the campers an hour to become occupied with their novelty toys or ball games, while the majority of counselors try to unwind, amidst the noise. Campers might also want to write a letter to their families during this time, which then gets sent to Zoe in the main office.

The second elective activity follows this. We're then alerted with the snack call—when everybody picks up a drink and a cookie or banana, to top up our energy levels. Then there's the third, fourth, and final activity on the compulsory agenda.

After all of that is shower-hour, which leads onto the first-call for supper. There's then an evening line-up after supper, where sports results, individual achievements and any other important announcements are addressed. Free-play time follows the evening line-up, which is when all the campers can freely roam around the sports complex and campsite, and the counselors on an OD are allocated to different stations, covering the entire premises. This means every camper is supervised during free-play.

The day concludes with an evening show and the two counselors from every bunkhouse who are on an OD are supervising their children all evening. This will include making sure all the kids are getting ready for bedtime, once they return to their bunkhouses after the evening show.

Every change of activity during the day is alerted with the brassy bugle signal, booming through the speakers around the campground. It's a noise that gets me out of bed in no time during the morning wake-up call. A clearer reading of the daily routine is as follows:

Time	Activity
7:30 a.m.	Reveille
7:45 a.m.	First-call
8:00 a.m.	Breakfast
8:45 a.m.	Line-up
9:00 a.m.	Clean-up
9:30 a.m.	Inspection
9:40 a.m.	1st Activity
10:25 a.m.	2nd Activity
11:10 a.m.	1st Elective
11:55 a.m.	Recall
12:15 p.m.	Lunch
12:45 p.m.	Rest-hour
1:50 p.m.	2nd Elective
2:40 p.m.	Snack
2:50 p.m.	3rd Activity
3:35 p.m.	4th Activity
4:20 p.m.	5th Activity
5:05 p.m.	Shower-hour
5:45 p.m.	First-call
6:00 p.m.	Dinner
6:30 p.m.	Line-up
6:45 p.m.	Free-play
7:40 p.m.	Recall
8:15 p.m.	Evening Show

All the campers are categorized by their ages, on both the girls' and boys' sides of the camp. This puts it into perspective of how massive the camp really is. First, there's the Freshmen division, which are the tiny, eight- to nine-year-olds. Following that is the Junior division. Then there's my group, which is the Middy division. By this age, most of the kids are very confident and mischievous. The next divisions are Navajo, Mohican, Cherokee, and Collegiate. Then there's the 16- to 17-year-olds, who are much larger in size, and many would easily be mistaken for a counselor if they wore a staff shirt. They are known as CIT, which stands for "counselors in training." They'll often help supervise the younger kids and learn the necessary attributes to become potential staff members for the following summer.

The program at the camp is diverse. It involves all the traditional sports, such as soccer, baseball, basketball, and lacrosse. There are also adventure sports, which include; the high ropes and low ropes courses, skateboarding, and mountain boarding. There's a catering facility that hosts a cookery program, and an art program with an indoor play area that's dedicated to Lego. Also, at the camp's disposal, there's a facility known as the "School of Rock," which houses the music program.

It's clear to see that there's something for every child at this summer camp. Every child has a unique experience. An example of the typical day for a camper can involve playing field hockey on the Astroturf, then moving up to the outdoor pavilion for the circus program, where they can practice flying trapeze or other acrobatic skills, using an aerial hammock. Then that camper could be walking down to Maple Lagoon for some banana boating. This may be followed by baking cookies, and finally having a game of softball on the baseball field. There are so many activities available to the children for their seven weeks here. It's impossible for the children not to enjoy themselves.

27

NEW UNDERSTANDINGS

After my third week at Camp Ace Invaders, there have been new understandings for me. Changing the way certain things are said is something, a first-timer Brit like me, has needed to adapt to at the summer camp. This includes saying; flashlight instead of torch, sneakers instead of trainers, chips instead of crisps, French fries instead of chips and soda instead of fizzy drink.

I also learn that the standards are very high, from the sports facilities, to the skilled personnel during the daily activities. When I observe the soccer coaches and the tennis team at work, I see that they're well-disciplined people, and are very engaging with the children. I now believe what Vince said regarding the process of recruiting people to meet these standards of professionalism—that the camp only hires the *best* people for the job.

I've learned a lot about the campers during their first couple of weeks, too. First, the smaller kids always want shoulder rides. This applies mainly to counselors of a relatively tall height, which, unfortunately, includes me. Once you give one kid a ride on your shoulders, there's no going back—numerous requests are sure to follow.

"Hey, can I have a ride on your shoulders?"

Shoulder rides are in popular demand, especially when I'm walking up the hills with my campers to either the baseball field or the mini wiffle ball stadium. That's *just what I need* to boost my energy levels for the busy days that are scheduled down to the minute. Doing this has given me backaches and increases my weariness, which isn't ideal when I'm on-duty overnight. An appointment with a massage therapist would be very welcomed.

Second, the children absolutely love playing with their diabolos and Rubik's cubes, even though many of them cannot solve their Rubik's cubes. And many seem to possess them simply for the craze.

In spite of that, I'm impressed by how skillful some of the kids are at playing with these obsessions, which occupies them unceasingly in their free time, to avoid any boredom. Some campers can solve their Rubik's cubes behind their backs, but I've never solved one in my life. Other campers perform tricks on the diabolo so effortlessly. I have a go at playing with a diabolo myself, and, to my surprise, find it very challenging. I cannot balance and spin the Chinese yo-yo on its string for any longer than 10 seconds, let alone launching the two-headed top into the air and catching the damn thing on its axle.

This is largely due to a lack of interest in playing with these specific toys as a child. I thought they were outdated. Right from my childhood, the gaming technology has been rapidly evolving. And regardless of playing with action figures in my imaginary world as a child, I was also engrossed in playing on video games from the age of six, which started with *Mario Kart* and *Streetfighter* on the Super Nintendo, to then *Crash Bandicoot* and *Tomb Raider* on the PlayStation One, and so on, through the many developments in game consoles, an endless supply of video game and advances in computer graphics every year. Seeing these campe being so content with their timeless toys that are rudimentary, compare to what kids can interact with nowadays, is something I find intriguing.

Third, most of the boys are amazing at basketball, especial compared to me and the average talent that England has to offer. I s children scoring a consecutive set of baskets all the time on the cour They have plenty of opportunities to practice and show off their abiliti for this sport, since the outdoor basketball courts are close by. The miniature basketballs and hoops inside the bunkhouse must equally he with their precision in scoring points.

Fourth, the Middy boys are unsurprisingly immature. One of t main things that illustrate this is their extreme obsession with jokes abc "sharting," which basically means farting that causes one to poo or, better suit this terminology, *shit* themselves. These jokes are allowed be said and heard because it simply makes the kids happy, even if th give the parents the epic eye roll.

I'm also aware that I'm working at a Jewish summer camp, but t is only because Bobby told me beforehand. The religion doesn't seem be pushed on anyone, and it's not obvious which campers come fr Jewish backgrounds.

With that said, there have been a few moments that have brou out the Jewish culture. These include the matzo-ball chicken soup traditional Jewish soup that's been served at supper. It doesn't look the most appetizing of foods. But I perceive it to be satisfying in ta though I may distinguish most food as yummy because of my increased hunger and need for calories this summer.

Another time, Brett uses his humor toward Judaism. On a couple of occasions, he pretends he's a "Jewish Santa," knowing full well that the majority of Jews don't celebrate Christmas. Yesterday I saw Brett sitting on the edge of his bed with Jasper, one of the campers, next to him.

"Ho-ho-ho. I'm Jewish Santa. What do you want for Hanukkah?" Brett said to Jasper.

Jasper quickly jumped off the bed in disapproval, as if he were walking away from a horrible stench in the room.

In the dining hall, it's undeniable that Camp Ace Invaders is full of enthusiastic people. This is evident during mealtimes, particularly when there are sudden announcements. As I arrive at the dining hall with Bunkhouse G every morning, we sit at one of the tables on the boy's side of the room. A head counselor in an uplifting voice announces when each division is next in line to collect their food on the self-service counters. We wait in our seats patiently until…

"Middy boys, you can now come up for your breakfast!"

These are the words that the children in my bunkhouse eagerly wait to hear and they dash up to the line with their trays. This is no different for the other mealtimes.

"It has been brought to my attention, boys and girls, that we have ICE-CREAM SANDWICHES FOR DESSERT TONIGHT!"

One of the head counselors announces this during supper, and it's met with an earsplitting cheer from across the dining hall. The campers glow with happiness.

"I hope you're all hungry tonight because we have CHOCOLATE FUDGE BARS FOR DESSERT TONIGHT!"

This is another announcement from a head counselor that's put through the speakers during a mealtime. These announcements generate a lot of food wastage. Many of the campers reject the rest of the savory meals they're currently eating at supper, because they're now fully devoted to the dessert that's been announced. Head counselors then march around the hall with giant cardboard boxes that are filled with the frozen desserts. The desserts are tossed out to the bundles of outstretched arms with open hands, like a crowd of spectators trying to grab a rock star at a concert.

Finally, once the day is almost complete, there's the evening show that's presented in the sports hall. Most nights feature the counselors. Other times, the campers are the stars of the show. One night, I witness a round-robin Ga-ga tournament that's only featuring the Middy division. Ga-ga is a game that has similar characteristics to dodgeball, though everyone is within an octagon that is bordered by benches. The aim of the game is to strike an opponent below the knee with the ball and the ball must be hit open-handed The game starts with a head counselor throwing the Ga-ga ball into the middle, while each player is touching a side of the octagon. After three bounces a player can make the first strike of the ball. Once a player is hit below the knee with the ball, they're eliminated. A player is also eliminated for knocking the ball out of the octagon. The game ends with the last player who remains in the octagon unhit. Unfortunately, none of the Bunkhouse G campers are victorious in this tournament.

Another evening show is a dating game, which mimics the outdated show, *Blind Date*, which was formerly presented on English TV by Cilla Black. A female or male chooses a series of questions for three members of the opposite sex, and these are responded with witty and somewhat romantic responses that must've been rehearsed to make the show entertaining. The person who asks the questions then gets to choose which one of the three people they'd like to *date*. Whether the couples of counselors or the couples of CITs that are matched on this show develop into actual relationships, or not, is unknown.

I soon realize, though, that if you spectate on a chair during an evening show in the sports hall, a kid is bound to fall asleep next to you, after using every ounce of energy they had for the daily activities. These are times of weariness for the campers. I want to disturb them in these moments, with a nudge, out of revenge for waking me up so early in the morning from their mini basketballs. But, instead, I act like I'm a caring older brother and allow them to catch up on their sleep, as I know that's essential for me, too.

28

THE DISMISSAL – EPISODE 1

I had spent an evening with Roxy and Megan. This was during orientation week. Roxy had ended up driving us to Walmart that night, so I could buy a cheap mobile phone, because my smartphone had stopped working, to my dismay. I believe this is due to water damage. The phone screen wouldn't always turn on. I repeatedly took the battery out and repositioned it into the phone again, and the screen would eventually light up and work, though only temporarily. I didn't want to persist with this hassle.

We also went to Sheetz on this particular night. Sheetz is a shop that's joined to a gas station and sells all types of sweet food. I bought Oreo ice-cream in a tub and some tangy flavored candy bars, called Air-Heads. We had a laugh and listened to Ed Sheeran on our way back to the campsite. But one thing that gave me some doubts about Roxy was when she was boasting about the times she had been speeding in her car while under the influence of alcohol, and even marijuana. She's only just reached the legal age to drink alcohol at 21. She has never been caught by the police during these careless acts, which made her a brilliant driver, in her deluded eyes.

By the following week, Megan had taken a dislike to Roxy, although they were both sharing a bunkhouse. Megan expressed to me that Roxy was argumentative and always wanted her own way in the bunkhouse. I do recall Roxy being resentful of another counselor in her bunkhouse, during orientation week, because they wanted to sleep on a bed that was prepared for one of the girl campers. I could understand why Roxy was complaining on that occasion, yet it seemed that she was getting into confrontations way too frequently, at least according to Megan. After orientation week, a relieved Megan told me that Roxy had moved to a different bunkhouse because she wasn't getting along with her colleagues.

Roxy, coincidently, had the same days off as me, though the day she gets fired is a day I spend at the Dickson City mall with a few of the male counselors whom I've gotten pally with. Roxy is the first staff member I hear of getting fired. Her brief service at Camp Ace Invaders is terminated because she was deemed too drunk to work with her children. She was questioned by a head counselor, during a suppertime, after returning to the campsite from her day off.

Robert was in my group that day, along with Louis and Max. None of us are keen on driving to the mall, so we spend most of the morning wandering around camp central, hoping to get an offer from someone to give us a lift. Eventually, while we're sitting on a bench by a basketball court, with the baking hot sun radiating over us, Becky comes to our rescue. She's the staff member who leads the health center. She offers to take us to Dickson City, which we accept. Becky must've been observing

us and wondering why we were sitting and not doing anything activ
the gorgeous weather.

After Becky kindly drives us to Dickson City, she tells us
another member of staff, belonging to the health center, will pick us u
approximately 4:30 p.m. that afternoon. We then have a meal at Bu
Wings, a restaurant dedicated to chicken wings and a selection of mil
painfully hot chili sauces. The sauce that I smother my chicken wi
medium hot, just enough to tingle my mouth. We also have a
around the mall, with no intention of shopping.

Later, we decide to leave the mall and trek over to Walmart,
than a mile away. After walking along some precarious, non-pedes
pathways, we arrive at Walmart and buy some snacks to take bac
camp. Max and I see Robert talking to Roxy by the checkout tills. W
decide to walk over to her. It turns out that Roxy is tipsy and has dr
to Walmart on her own. Roxy starts ranting to us that she was with c
counselors earlier in the day doing cliff diving, and it was there tha
was drinking alcohol.

The situation worsens when she claims that police officers
actually spotted her and the group drinking on a clifftop. It's stric
non-diving and non-drinking zone. It's a zone that I'll now be avoic
Roxy tells us that everyone doing the cliff diving had scurried off w
the officers were noticed and parted ways with her. It wouldn't I
been surprising if she invited herself along to the cliff div
unannounced.

Roxy has a busted lip with disheveled hair (compared to her u
tied back hair). I gather that this is from her explaining how she slip

and face planted onto a rock, while escaping out of the area. This must've also been caused by her alcoholic intoxication, as well as her immaturity. Roxy then asks if any of us want a lift back to the summer camp. Reluctantly, I say that we're going to walk back to the mall.

At around 4:30 p.m., Louis, Robert, and I get a lift back from the entrance of the shopping mall with a staff member, called Sally. She picks us up in the iconic Camp Ace Invaders minibus. Max surprisingly goes back to camp with Roxy.

Later, I bump into Max at the campsite. It turns out that Roxy stopped off at a liquor store and bought a vodka slush puppy drink, which they shared on the journey back. In contrast to Roxy's perceptible level of drunkenness, Max is sober and he halts anymore discussion of today's antics.

After supper that evening, I hear that Roxy has been fired, and was told to pack her luggage. On the night of Roxy's departure, most of the girls in the counselors' lounge embrace each other with hugs, feeling ecstatic and relieved that Roxy is gone. Witnessing this makes it seem like it was the correct decision for Roxy to leave.

29

THE DISMISSAL - EPISODE 2

Baxter will always be known for his phobia of dolphins. He spoke about having a scuba dive in Hawaii, and that he saw these dolphins in the water that looked sinister and showed a willingness to attack him, but he *somehow* escaped fatality. This story has spread around the camp like the wildfire, until most campers and counselors, particularly in the Middy division, were shrieking dolphin-like noises at Baxter.

"Ehh! Ehh! Ehh!" screeched many kids, during line-ups.

It's safe to say that Baxter wasn't impressed. These noises went on continuously until his final days at camp. I remember a counselor asking Baxter:

"Would you rather get into a tank full of sharks, piranhas, or dolphins?"

To everyone's amazement, Baxter didn't answer dolphins.

He was one of the bulkier counselors, with the build of a professional wrestler, and rising a few inches taller than me. On occasions, the Middy boys' division had to wait within the confines of the gymnasium, before rain showers subsided and activities resumed. These were times when many campers swarmed around Baxter's presence.

Campers jumped onto his back, in attempt to take the big man down to the floor, acting out how armies conquered Godzilla and King Kong in the movies. The children also tormented Brett in this fashion, as he's also of a heavy build and can withstand the weight of many kids combined.

Having this attention from the kids appeared to make Baxter seem playful. For instance, when he play-fought by body slamming the kids onto the foam mats, they got great enjoyment out of it. This play-fighting went on for about 20 minutes at a time, until a new activity was initiated for the Middy boys.

During a Middy boys' trip to the local state park, I vividly remember stopping my Frisbee throwing on the sandy bank to watch Baxter in the lake. All you could see was Baxter's head poking out of the water with multiple kids weighing him down, while making dolphin noises.

"AHHH!" roared Baxter.

All of a sudden, Baxter speared out of the water, like the Incredible Hulk, hurling all the kids into the water, who were wrestling him. It was hilarious to witness.

A couple of days after this, I'm on my day off, and decide to take Baxter's offer in giving me and Robert a ride in his car into Dickson City to have another look around the mall. Our sense of direction is poor, and it takes several U-turns in rural areas near the summer camp to get on track. But it ends up being an enjoyable day, which includes us going to a Mexican food bar and eating burritos with a shared portion of tortilla chips with melted cheese on top, and with different sauces, including spicy salsa and chipotle sauce.

It's only the next day, during the evening line-up, when I see a different side to Baxter. Most of the counselors are waiting patiently with their campers by a tetherball post, next to the American flag. This is where all of the line-ups take place on the boys' side. Simon, a camper who took a liking to Baxter, was one of the kids who always flocked to wherever Baxter was standing, especially when the play-fighting commenced. Before this particular evening line-up, though, Simon is hanging around Baxter and kicking him repeatedly in the shins to get his attention. Baxter is deliberately ignoring the boy.

This continues for a couple of minutes until Baxter, suddenly and ferociously, rugby tackles Simon to the ground and presses both of his monstrous hands onto Simon's fragile chest for several agonizing seconds. Baxter releases his hold after being restrained by a group of counselors. Simon is on the ground wheezing. Tears are trickling down his face, and he's short of breath for a good minute; but it seems like an eternity. It's a very awkward moment on boys' side. I intently watch Baxter. His eyes are bulging with fury, and he's seething with Simon lying helplessly below. Some of our colleagues are comforting Simon, while others are dead silent in shock over what had just happened.

Roughly 30 minutes after this, we've been dismissed from line-up, and the head counselors are totally oblivious to what occurred earlier Then Simon, with a red, puffy face, runs up to head counselor, Randy and reports what had happened.

Later that evening, I'm lifting weights in the gym. I see genera counselor, Kenny, enter the gym, and he lets me in on the gossip from hi bunkhouse. Kenny says that while Bunkhouse F was relaxing after the line-up, Simon walked up to Baxter in the bunkhouse and revealed wha he had said to Randy.

"You're lucky you ain't fired because I told them you were a good counselor."

That comment proves that Simon thinks very highly of Baxter, even underneath the recent horror. Kenny says that Baxter didn't even acknowledge or respond to the boy. Not even an apology was made. Kenny adds that Baxter has to leave camp for what he did. He thinks that he'll certainly be going home.

Then, an hour later, news comes in from the counselors' lounge that Baxter has, indeed, been fired. I don't know why Baxter acted so appallingly. There were better solutions to the problem at the line-up. Baxter firstly needed to stay cool and calm, and to keep his strong emotions in check. He could've then given one warning (about the kicking in the shins), making it clear to Simon that his behavior was inappropriate and unwelcome. Simon could've been threatened with a report to Vince, or worse, the parents, which is often effective in diffusing a situation in Bunkhouse G. Instead, Baxter let Simon's undesirable behavior continue until a meltdown occurred for everyone to see, and that was unprofessional and a breach of contract. In all honesty, Baxter seemed like a nice guy who you could have a genuine conversation with. But his actions that day weren't acceptable.

30

THE CURRENT SHENANIGANS

As the weeks go on, the family atmosphere at Camp Ace Invaders continues to build. I also start to notice things that *really* bug us counselors. They come from our cunning, troublesome campers.

Firstly, most of our campers can't fold their clothes properly, and *we counselors* are the ones doing the refolding. This is especially noticeable on laundry day, after two head counselors skid to a screeching stop in their golf carts outside our bunkhouse and they chuck three large drawstring sacks of washed and dried laundry onto the porch. Everyone's washing is all topsy-turvy together. As there are no elective activities on Wednesdays, we sort through the laundry as a replacement in that time.

It takes a good part of an hour to place each piece of clothing onto the beds of the correct campers and counselors. Then Robert and I usually demonstrate to the campers the art of folding a piece of clothing and we encourage them to perfect it, so they can help because, as Bobby urges in the line-ups, "Teamwork makes the dream work!"

Secondly—and we already realized this long ago—all kids have brought too much clothing with them. This means their laundry has to be folded really small so that it can all fit into their cubbies. Cramming all of the clothing in such an organized and smart way is an art form. We reiterate how the cubby area resembles a sports store, with an endless supply of sportswear from all the professional teams that are favored by these 10- to 11-year-olds.

Besides that, we counselors don't approve of campers going into the cubby area and carelessly climbing up onto the shelves and pulling down whatever clothing they want to wear. When they do this, it results in a pile of laundry to crash to the floor and *we counselors* have to reorganize the shelves. We'd prefer it if the campers tell us their choices on what to wear so that we can carefully pluck out the clothing for them.

Third, there's tetherball, which is frequently played during free-play. I routinely get frustrated, trying to drag campers away from the tetherball post when they should be en route to their next timetabled activities. The Middy boys are enthralled when the volleyball is swinging clockwise or counterclockwise on the tetherball posts, depending on what direction the campers are whacking the ball. They cannot take their eyes away from these sights when the ball gets in motion, just like when a basketball is flying around the courts and swooshing into the net. When a tetherball match has finished, though, it's always met by shrieks of: "Next available!" This call means that a kid wants to be next in line for the upcoming tetherball match. If I had a dollar for every time I heard those words, then I'd be a very rich man this summer.

Fourth, the campers usually want cans of soda at the most inopportune times—this is typically toward the end of shower hour. This means that one of *us counselors* has to go off with a group of sugar-craving campers to the head office, where they can receive up to two dollars a day, which is enough to choose a soda from the vending machine. This process can delay us from entering the dining hall for supper. Plus, the sodas produce a sugar rush that turns the kids hyper, making them more of a challenge to assemble for supper—and I become increasingly hungry and irritable.

The frustrations don't stop there, so we start to make some rules. Very little help is offered by the campers during clean-up. The same three or four kids are always the most helpful, and, for their good deeds, they're allowed first access to the showers during shower hour. Many of the kids in the bunkhouse complain that they never get to go to the shower station early, though this is a consequence for their lack of effort in clean-ups, in addition to their poor behavior over the course of the day. We may also keep a kid in *bunkhouse detention,* instead of roaming freely outside during rest-hour, or put a camper on a *soda ban* for the day.

In the mornings, once everyone makes their beds, each camper is given their own assignment for clean-up. A small group is urged to grab a broom, dustpan, and brush to clear away any mess on the main floor of the bunk. Two or three are urged to help a counselor tidy up the clothing piled up in the cubbies, while others grab mops and a bucket to clean the floor below the showers. Whoever is left is encouraged to sweep the porch that forms the entrance of the bunkhouse. Our orders to the campers are usually received by hesitant smiles until they reluctantly do their chores, and half-heartedly by most.

There are also plenty of card games at camp, which come in handy during the rainy days. Many kids are particularly obsessed with "Magic" cards, which feature wizards that employ spells, and creatures c different strengths and powers. This is similar to Yu-Gi-Oh and Pokémon. As a child, I was a Pokémon fanatic.

Rainy days are the worst part at camp, and they've happened on more occasions than I had hoped. Rain means longer times in the bunkhouse, or in enclosed areas, such as the circus pavilion, gymnasium, or canteen. The longer this persists, the more bored, restless and whinier the campers become. Luckily, the rain has never lasted a whole day, and most scheduled activities are unaffected.

A countless number of activities are organized, not only by the specialist counselors, as per the schedule, but also by the kids in the bunkhouses when they have time to themselves. One of the games is called "taps," and Bunkhouse G uses the roof of the bunkhouse to play it. Taps is played with a Ga-ga ball, which is essentially a rubber kickball. The bunkhouse has a pitched roof, and the game is started once the kids form a line on the porch below it. The first one in the line throws the ball onto the roof. Then each kid, in turn, tries to keep the ball on the roof by tapping it back up when it falls off the edge. Both feet have to be off the ground during contact with the ball. If a kid messes up then they're eliminated, and it continues that way until there's an eventual winner.

Another game that's played inside the bunkhouse, with a high level of stupidity, is "elimination." It starts with all the campers crowded together inside the main room of the bunkhouse. Then a camper puts a small rubber ball in their hand. The camper with the ball then launches it at the inside of our front door, to make it rebound back and hit one of the campers. They're basically using themselves as human bowling pins. If the ball bounces off the door and hits the ground first, then the other players are able grab the ball and re-throw it at the door. If a kid is able to catch the ball then the thrower has to touch the door before being "pegged" (struck with a thrown rubber ball) to avoid elimination. If a kid gets hit by the ball rebounding off the door, then they also need to touch the door without being pegged (to avoid elimination). Fortunately, from what I recall on my watch, no one ever got upset or injured during these games. But I'm now urging them not to play this under my supervision—for their safety, as well as our poor door.

Times like these make me realize that the campers have a lack of awareness for the possible consequences of unwise acts. They thrive on the element of risk. Just like little me and friends whom I played with on the streets of our neighborhood. At one stage, we could be seen with loaded spud guns (with a potato in our pocket for extra ammo) that we chased each other with. That was until someone cried, after receiving a brilliant head shot, and the parents complained. But owning up to mistakes like this enabled moral development. This was before the media promoted a *cotton wool* parenting culture, deeming it unsafe for kids to climb trees, build dens out of bamboo sticks and fallen branches, and stay out on their bikes after dark.

On other occasions this summer, the kids get me running after them in tag games. Or they may automatically nominate me in "follow the leader," which is when they walk the way I walk, make the same motions I make and say the same things I say.

A summer camp is a place that's full of many silly games. But camp has taught me that if a game makes the kids happy, keep playing that game, even if you're exhausted. Those laughs and smiles make every camper's summer.

31

EVENING ENTERTAINMENT

The final event on a typical day is the evening show. Lately, there's been a bingo night, where the kids got a board each with numbers. They desperately scan their numbers, hoping to eliminate the quantity as quickly as possible. Some of the campers have counselors watching over them, for support. Kids scream "bingo" when all their numbers are filled, and those winners skip up to the stage to receive their rewards. Most of the time, the rewards consist of a cookie or pizza night for the bunkhouse, or a movie night. Some of the luckier campers got singular rewards that even I would be delighted with, such as a pair of Doctor Dre headphones.

Another evening show has been the boys' lip-sync battle. The stars of this night's show included the male head counselors, who lip-sync to the well-known pop music of the past decade. One act was when three head counselors, including Randy and Beefy, lip-sync the song "All the Single Ladies" by Beyoncé. The three confident men on stage wear girly attire. They wear high heels, tight denim shorts and whatever else that's lent to them from their female counterparts. It was bewildering for me to witness, though squeals of wolf-whistling could be heard from the female counselors. The dance moves are unorthodox, to say the least, with twerking and slut-dropping, which would be very appealing Beyoncé herself were on stage doing it. But with the opposite se performing, it's just hilarious, and definitely cringe-worthy.

The winners of the battle, though, were a group of CITs imitating th "Party Rock Anthem" by LMFAO. It was brilliantly choreographed, wit not a moonwalk, head-spin or lip movement out of place. Th mesmerized crowd had smiles from ear-to-ear, as they clapped and sar along to the music. Later into the performance, the entertainers the brought out fire extinguishers from backstage and sprayed the caniste all around the stage, until a white mist covers them. This act ge laughter, as well as great applause.

A hypnotist is the star of another evening. He hypnotizes a doze counselors, who are audacious to nominate themselves. Two of th counselors on stage with the hypnotist are Brett and Megan's best frien Erica. They all sit along a row of plastic classroom chairs, facing th watchful crowd. The hypnotist magically sends them all into hypnos with the click of his fingers. Their eyes close, and they becom motionless. They only respond to the commands given by the hypnoti and this causes them to perform amusing acts. They pretend to b driving a car. They then become emotional by believing that they've ju ran over a puppy. At one stage, they erotically sniff each other shoulders, with not a care in the world.

Despite the hilarity from the audience, this show receives criticis from some counselors, who don't believe that real hypnotism was bein performed. Everyone in Bunkhouse G questions Brett later that nigl about the show, and Brett confesses that he can't remember anything th

130

happened. He looks truthful. Whether this is the case or not is unknown. One thing is for certain—it was hysterical to watch.

In my spare evenings on the campsite, I sometimes hang out at the counselors' lounge. I've also mingled around campfires at lakeside. There, Megan introduced me to the traditional, sugary campfire delight known as s'mores, consisting of melting marshmallow and chocolate spread. This is sandwiched between two graham crackers, which are the American alternative to digestive biscuits. In spite of the taste, you have to be careful not to leave a sticky mess on your hands or clothing.

I also socialize with Gavin on nights off, whom I met on the first night. Due to us both supporting the same English football team, we've discussed about Spurs' ambitions for the upcoming football season. We're hopeful that the club chairman, Daniel Levy, will allow our manager to purchase some world-class footballers. Gavin is an archery specialist, and it just so happens that I'm his assistant for one of the daily electives, to supervise those campers who have opted to partake in archery. There's plenty of chit-chat with Gavin, in addition to the sudden yells of caution at certain kids:

"Stand behind the white line until everyone has finished firing their arrows!"

This has been addressed to campers when they try to prematurely collect their arrows in one of the three 20-yard lanes, while others are still aiming at their targets. Fortunately, none of the kids have ended up becoming another sad story for Vince.

32

A HEALTHY MIND

As I think for a moment, I realize how the environment at Camp Ac
Invaders has been so new and revolutionary to me this summer. Thi
environment in the summertime portrays a major difference between th
lifestyle in America and England, especially for children. Summer camp
are a tradition in America, so American people are familiar with th
system and how the family dynamics change for the summer.

American parents take their children to summer camps for a respite
while they carry on with their responsibilities for the businesses the
work for. A 10-year-old version of me would've been terrified at th
thought of spending two months away from my parents, but this is
way of life in the U.S. The campers get used to it.

My thoughts then change to the irony of how, before this summer,
constantly used technology and the Internet to connect with a summe
camp, but now that I'm at a summer camp, I'm unplugged fror
everything I was so reliant on in England. No Facebook, no Skype, n
emails, and no text messages—I've been enjoying life without it.

Consumerism has reached epic proportions, and people ge
disgruntled simply by not owning the latest gadget. On the flip side, a
this summer camp, we're disconnected from consumerism and the worl

of social media. The truth is that the society outside of the summer camp is disconnected from life. We use artificial light and air conditioning indoors more than the daylight and fresh air of the outdoors. We no longer know how to live without cars, phones, computers, and our favorite shops. We only act naturally when we eat, sleep, excrete, and roam the countryside away from urban areas.

It's been refreshing to live away from the Internet. It's also been refreshing to be disconnected from this materialistic world, and the media that's full of negativity and violence. Vince and Marie remind all of us in a talk that you have to *disconnect to connect*, which is also ironic, since an online statistic reveals that 80% of camps (including Camp Ace Invaders) use social networking sites for marketing purposes.

Nonetheless, conversations on a text message or Facebook Messenger aren't meaningful. In order to create real friendships with people, you need to have a face-to-face conversation and do things with them, like going on adventures and participating in physical activities. Life's about making memories!

I then think about my health. The anxiety that I was battling with prior to this experience has subsided, and I'm becoming less conscious of it. I'm starting to feel like myself again. Instead of not knowing who I am as a person and how to follow the path of adult life, I'm starting to see through the eyes of *the real me*.

I believe that the telephone counseling was helpful in making this work. I have used the techniques suggested by Sophie from iTalk when I remember to, such as taking deep and controlled breaths and dismissing any negative thoughts that I may have been thinking. I also believe that having a purpose and being active in taking responsibility for others has taken my mind off my apprehensive thoughts. This is probably the key to happiness. Whether the changes I've made with Sophie's help will be maintained over the long term is unknown. But becoming more active in doing things I like and being purpose-driven will hopefully give me a healthy mind for the foreseeable future.

33

VISITING DAY

Visiting day is the halfway point for the campers. It's when their family members enter the campground in their droves to visit their loved ones and check how *the camp life* is going for them this summer. When the kids first meet their fathers and mothers again, it's emotionally intense for them. They embrace one another with hugs and kisses, and like clockwork, every boy breaks down into tears. You can see how much family means to them, and how homesick they clearly are at their tender ages, even though this hasn't been their first summer away from their families.

The one criticism I have about visiting day is that the parents bring way too much candy. And it's not just candy, but also cakes, potato chips, giant cookies, and other luxuries. The kids in my bunkhouse get spoiled by gifts, such as extra pairs of shoes and novelty toys to play with, even though they already have lots at their disposal. I notice Ethan receiving an extra pair of LeBron James shoes. Since becoming a "legal alien" in America, I realize that these shoes are a big deal, since they're branded by the very successful and famous basketball player, LeBron James. Instead of saying thank you, Ethan says that the shoes are the wrong color, and that he doesn't want to wear them.

Without seeming disappointed in Ethan's rejection of the expensive footwear, his mother responds by saying that she'll exchange them at the shoe store for the right color, and that she'll have them waiting for him at home when he gets back. I don't hear Ethan say *thank you*, in response. These kids have so much to be grateful for. They have footwear for every single sport at camp, including studded boots for soccer, LeBron James shoes, or something of similar value, for basketball, and turf shoes for baseball. And some of them have more than one pair of footwear for a sport. In the storage room of the cabin, we have lacrosse sticks, baseball bats, basketballs, American footballs, and tennis rackets to suit the various activities on camp and most of these are brand spanking new. The shiny, glossy look to the equipment is a giveaway for this.

After I finish my morning as a supervisory assistant at the waterfront area, I stroll around the campus with Robert, Megan and Erica. As we wander, I see many families in high spirits. I can see families swimming, amidst all the inflatables at the waterfront, and other families having picnics in the grassy areas. Also, families are participating in the mini wiffle ball stadium at the top of the hill, which is available to them today.

I can't help but notice that many of the mums appear to look younger than the dads, and are unquestionably the better looking of the couples. I overhear a group of counselors complimenting the mums, in secrecy.

"Wow, did you see Noah's mum? She's hot."

"Dude, Scott's mum is a fine-looking woman, too!"

Despite that, it's undeniable that the parents show compassion and love to their little ones on visiting day. They also want to know how their kids behave within the bunkhouse. Parents have asked us: "How has my son been?"

Instead of telling them about the constant torment that their little terrors have caused over the weeks, I automatically find myself replying politely: "He's been fine. He seems to be enjoying himself."

On two separate occasions, I get a carbon-copy response:

"No. How has my son *really* been?"

That's when I realize that the aging fathers and mothers have lived through years of what I've only been experiencing for a few weeks. Rather than disappointing the parents, *I hide the fact* that most of the kids don't settle down to sleep until midnight. You and the other counselor are sailing the ship alone on an OD night against the shit storm that the campers create in the bunkhouse. It's either sink or swim while they make silly noises in bed and play with their flashlights. Campers will happily see you sink under the pressure. Fortunately, the discipline enforced on my OD nights have prevailed and the bunkhouse eventually becomes ghost-quiet. Then you have the standard six hours of sleep, at best, before another strenuous day shift begins. But *I hide the fact* that their sons jump out of bed early in the morning and play with their indoor basketballs before the bugle is alarming everyone for the official wakeup call. I also *hide the fact* that they curse regularly in conversation with one another, even when they're in close proximity to the counselors.

Instead, I report that they can make life difficult during shower-hour and when we're supposed to be tidying the bunkhouse each morning, which is true. But I add that "they're generally good kids," which is met by suspicious nods of approval.

By the time late afternoon comes around, the families start to depart. The emotions of this morning are all seen and heard again. Some kids cling to their parents in their cries. Others are shouting in sadness:

"Please don't go… I want you to stay!"

The unhappiness from these departures could make it seem like I'm a bad counselor and not helping the kids to have a great summer. But then Robert, Brett, Nate, or I put an arm around a camper's shoulder and try to distract them from their saddened moods. The campers have all navigated their way to good friendships with counselors and other campers without their mum and dad. And it's not just about the kids having fun on the soccer or baseball field or learning to play the drums. It's also about them becoming more independent and feeling really good about themselves. It's about them trying new things that they thought they couldn't do and succeeding at them. We're here, as counselors, to help them through this process.

It also makes me think back to my family, and whether I should be Skyping them again soon. I've spoken to them on three separate occasions already, in the counselors' lounge. It's nice to see my family's faces on the other side of the world, and I get to see Rosie the cat, when Mum lifts her up to the camera.

However, every time I interact with them, we keep getting interrupted by the weak signal, as I'm within a remote environment amidst the mountains of Pennsylvania. The weak signal has made me feel frustrated during Skype conversations, and the hindrance of this distorts the true reflection of my overseas experience. Next time I have a conversation with my family, I'll let them know that I'll call them again on my travels after camp. I provide updates of my experience to my brothers over Facebook anyway, so at least there's still contact.

Soon after all the parents leave the campsite, the kids are lying on their beds, occupied with their piles of goodies. This raises their spirits, and it seems like a Christmas morning to them. *We counselors* are just flies on the wall.

34

THE CANDY GODS

There was a counselor meeting in orientation week, on the subject of how sly the children are about stashing their food they receive on visiting day. This meeting also brought to my awareness that the kids will eat as much as possible in the next 24 hours, after the parents leave; because they know they'll have their food taken away by the "candy gods."

Candy gods are basically head counselors dressed up in costumes to suit a theme, who snatch as much candy as they can from every cabin. The candy gods do this because (a) leftover food will attract unwelcome wildlife into the cabins, (b) some of the foods may contain nuts, which can trigger an anaphylactic shock for those with nut allergies, and (c) overindulging in candy is obviously unhealthy for the campers, and won't do them any favors in the vigorous activities that they do each day.

I watch it all happen. The parents brought too much candy and other sugary foods on visiting day. A sugary smell develops in the bunkhouse that's pungent and gets quite nauseating after a while. That evening, the kids eat lashings of their food before and after suppertime. Faces then turn pale in the latter part of the evening, until they eventually vomit. Fortunately, the vomiting occurs into the toilet bowl, and not on any of the bedsheets or flooring of Bunkhouse G.

By the next day, rumors come flooding in about counselors receiving money from some of the parents. This is probably because the campers have praised particular counselors in letters to their parents. This gesture from the parents has been strongly discouraged by Vince and Bobby. We're supposed to reject any offers of money. But Steve and Gavin have arrogantly admitted to picking up 50 dollars each, and other sums between 20 and 70 dollars are rumored to have been collected by other colleagues. This must've come as welcoming bonus pay for those counselors, considering that we're making no more than a dollar an hour when we're on-duty. To my knowledge, no counselors in Bunkhouse G were offered any money, though we each received a box of Swedish Fish sweets from the thoughtfulness of Dustin's parents.

On the day after visiting day, though, several head counselors dress up in inflatable dinosaur costumes and steal as much food as possible. I don't see this happen, as the head counselors do it surreptitiously, while the campers are having timetabled activities. This must've taken a lot of skill when you're a clumsy T-Rex with baby arms. But supposedly, the dinosaurs are seen by some very dismayed and equally frightened campers, who witness the silent invasions right in front of their eyes.

35

DROPPING LIKE FLIES

In the space of a week, a number of counselors depart in quick succession. Two counselors mysteriously leave due to family reasons. Then Milton is next. Everyone seems to think that he's the oldest counselor here. This is because of the way he carries himself. Plus, his receding hairline and his bulbous eyes staring at others through his thick glasses only contributes to this perception of him. He resembles the Simon Cowell look, with his cream-colored trousers raised to a high waistline, only to be tightened by his flabby build. It's eventually found out, through social media research that he's, in fact, a 22-year-old, and a year younger than me.

It doesn't take long for people to comment on how creepy he acts Other people's encounters with Milton suggest behavior that is very outlandish. Brett hears Milton saying that he's going to marry one of the Hungarian cooks, while pointing her out during a mealtime at the dining hall. He also sent the strangest-looking wink to Erica while crunching or a blueberry, before attempting to make awkward conversation.

On the night of July the 4th, after the phenomenal fireworks displa on the lacrosse field, to celebrate Independence Day, Milton is seer honking the horn of his car outside Bunkhouse C with high beams on.

not only looked extremely bizarre, it could've also been a sackable offense.

In the end, Milton isn't fired. Instead, he resigns. This is due to a mixture of complaints from campers that he's generally a poor counselor. Ben is a counselor who's been living in Bunkhouse C with Milton. After Milton's resignation, Ben tells me that Milton did nothing productive in his bunkhouse and would often be slumped on his bed for long periods, even when he was on-duty.

A day later, after supper, I hear a group of counselors discussing about Blake. It dawns on me that I hadn't seen Blake for a couple of days and I wondered, what could've possibly happened to him? Blake did peculiar things when I was in his company, such as when he would clout me firmly on the back or jab me in the stomach, like a boxer sparring. I found this bothersome in the beginning, and could've easily started a fight with him, though I soon realized that this was his way of acknowledging his male associates.

Blake also used the type of humor that would single out someone. A prime example of this was when he laughed at Steve, a general counselor from Scotland, with ginger hair and freckled skin. A few weeks ago, Steve got heavily sunburnt on the face and neck, resembling a beetroot. Blake named Steve, "sun-stroke Steve," and from that point on, Steve's nickname stuck onto camp soil, like gum (or dog muck) onto the bottom of one's shoe.

The reason that I haven't seen Blake, though, is because he got fired. Certain people reported negatively of him to the head counselors. He supposedly spanked a couple of his campers with a towel after they left

the shower area. I hear this through Greg, who has been living i
Bunkhouse A with Blake.

In spite of Greg telling me that his Cherokee campers found th
towel hitting humorous, and were always plotting pranks at Blake
expense, this information poses a different reflection when it reache
Vince, Marie and Bobby. This behavior cannot be condoned an
undermines the professionalism of his job title.

When I talk to Gavin about the news, he tells me that he had a hear
to-heart conversation with Blake one day at camp. Blake told Gavin tha
he's not having the best time at camp because of his *insecurities*. Mayb
his lightheartedness and antics were all a façade and just a way to try an
fit in.

Another person to leave is Matt, who always appeared to be
popular and charismatic individual at camp. He leaves in a very abrup
and devastating way, which happens during his day off. The day o
involved the precarious cliff diving activity. It's reported that Matt ha
fallen onto a rock from a considerable height. His footing slipped, and h
hand grip weakened, while he was climbing the cliff after a daring dive.

Consequently, he has sustained damage to his spine. The extent o
the injury is unknown, but he's rushed to a nearby hospital and we a
hope he has a speedy recovery. This elucidates how unsafe this off-dut
activity can be.

36

HOMESICKNESS

Ethan tends to say crazy things. This usually occurs when he's upset about being homesick, and once asked the question:

"What if Adolf Hitler is still alive?"

"He would be too old to be alive now, Ethan," I said in response.

This summer, he's also been concerned about the terrorist group, "ISIS," and I recall him asking Robert:

"What if ISIS terrorists are hiding underground and poke out of rabbit holes and sniper me while I'm away from my family?"

Despite the poor political knowledge, Ethan and other campers have to be lectured by me and Robert. We say that this military group won't randomly attack anyone here at this camp, and all their families are safe.

We avoid sharing any further details with the kids, such as the fact that this group, formed in Iraq and Syria, could be planning to cause more murderous chaos and terror that we've already seen in the news. The world is a scary place at the moment, with the uncertainty of when a terrorist attack may occur again. But the kids don't need to be perturbed about it. We reassure the children that they're in a safe place.

I wonder where the kids get these stories from. Are they overhearing inappropriate comments from the idiocy of adults? Or could it be a case of children seeing and hearing the easily accessible toxicity that's in the mass media? We now live in a world where, not just adults, but children have constant access to electronics and social media. This also means access to rumors in the news that can bring fear into people.

However, at the summer camp, the campers are so occupied with activities with their friends all day, such as hitting a home run in baseball or jumping into the lake. This avoids them finding negative news stories, as well as snapping, posting and using their favorite apps on the phone. They are unplugged from the distractions of their devices and instead learn from the natural world around them.

Nonetheless, there are many other moments when the campers experience feelings of homesickness, especially at night. They approach us with flat faces, the light completely drained out of them. I then find myself discussing with the campers about what's been troubling them. We talk and actively listen to the kids in a quiet place when this happens, usually on the porch outside of the bunkhouse.

Sometimes homesickness lasts 10 or 20 minutes. Other times it lasts the best part of an hour. Nine times out of ten, it'll be about missing their family. But they find the talks reassuring. Kids just want to be listened to.

It's our duty as counselors to make sure that the kids feel like they're living in a fun and supportive environment. Preventing any negative thoughts by tackling homesickness is pivotal in making that happen. It's part of being a counselor at a summer camp.

37

THE SLEEPWALKER

Terence has displayed bizarre behavior at night, which has freaked the hell out of Bobby and other staff at camp. Apparently, last summer, Terence crept out of his bed, walked up to another boy's bed, and was teetering over him, like a terrifying character from a horror film, possessed by a demon.

He stared at the boy for one disturbingly long minute, and then turned his head and stared at the counselor who had spotted him. The counselor called his name out, but Terence didn't move. Terence then stared back down at the kid who was sleeping, before slowly rotating back to his bed and sleeping again. Nothing escalated further that night—to everyone's relief.

Something happened again this summer, during a night when I'm having trouble sleeping. I can hear Terence suddenly shoot out of his bed.

"No… No! No!" he mutters as he stands up.

His eyes appear to be open. Then he rushes toward the door.

"What are you doing, Terence?" I question abruptly.

He stops for a moment and gives me a glassy stare.

"Go back to bed," I say.

Terence slowly walks back to his bed in a suspicious way. By this point, Nate has sat up in bed, looking very perplexed. Terence then crouches and rustles a carrier bag below his bed. I'm in a muddle, not knowing what to say or do, aside from keeping my eyes fixed onto Terence. I have the concern that he may carry out something dangerous or that he may run away on an escapade.

He's then standing up and tipping himself over Stan's bed. He slowly rubs his hands together like an evil villain, about to commit a crime.

"Terence, go back to bed!" I shout, which wakes a few campers.

He slowly backs away to his own bed and thankfully settles to sleep. I really hope that this'll be a one-off occurrence.

38

THE EXCURSIONS

On several occasions, the kids are able to enjoy day trips away from the campground, and these are stressful moments for *us counselors*, who look out for their campers attentively throughout the day. On one excursion, we're spectators of a baseball match, hosted at the stadium of the Scranton Rail-Riders. I'm assigned to Terence, Jasper, Malcolm, and Ethan during this outing, and I'm apprehensive about my responsibilities. The baseball match is incredibly boring, doesn't spark any interest in me, and provokes the children to wander the premises.

Each kid is allowed to spend 20 dollars on an outing, which means that they frequently stroll off to food outlets for snacks, as well as toilet breaks. It's a difficult task to assemble the kids together in their groups, because they also want to socialize with their friends. And sometimes they just want to deliberately be a pain in the backside. I'm surprised I haven't lost my voice by the time we leave the stadium.

Another trip, which most kids loved, is the Camel Beach Waterpark. We encounter many thrilling slides, though Jasper is not as keen as the other boys, which means that me or Kenny (the other counselor in my group) were required to stay as a spectator with Jasper for many of the slides that the other boys find enthralling.

The prospect of losing a kid or having a camper abducted by a stranger scares all of the counselors. Another fear that could easily have become reality was that of a child experiencing an allergic reaction to a food they purchase. A common allergy, that Vince announces as a *message of awareness,* prior to these outings, is nut allergies. This allergy has caused great trauma to members of the camp in previous years, with the effects of an anaphylactic shock being a possibility for unfortunate victims. Fortunately, I experience no heart-wrenching emergencies on my watch. I cross my fingers that this good fortune continues throughout the summer.

There have been staff members that may have found this summer too much work with not enough free time, or they just like their nights off with other counselors instead of being with the kids. This has caused staff members to underperform in their role, leave through a lack of enjoyment, or, like Roxy, get fired because they're not matching up with the balance of the *work hard, play hard* lifestyle.

However, in addition to my nights by the campfire, or in The Chasers, as being time away from the kids, I've also experienced offsite trips with other counselors I've befriended. These are on occasions when I've been entitled to an overnight pass, to somewhere off-campus and we can have the following day to ourselves, too. The bookings for where we stay are organized by us. We contribute a percentage of our earnings to these overnighters, which we collect from Zoe in the main office. We have permission and freedom from Camp Ace Invaders to make our own decisions.

It's nice to unwind and to forget about the kids. I have two enjoyable overnighters with a group of both male and female counselors. The first overnight stay is in New York City, in an apartment, and it makes me feel like I'm on an episode of the famous sitcom, *Friends*. It's also my first encounter with the bright lights of "the Big Apple." This is a taste of what's to come, as I'm planning New York City to be my first destination in my month of travel after camp.

My other stopover is at a lake house. We're very pleased again with what we manage to rent, after some research over the Internet. It's an expansive, three-story property consisting of a surround-sound system, a pool table, a giant flat-screen TV in the lounge, and a Jacuzzi. We feel like we're living the celebrity lifestyle and drink ourselves silly, on pre-bought alcohol, consisting of cans of Four Loko—caffeinated alcoholic beverages that are fruity in flavor and that really pack a punch!

I passed out on a sofa in the early hours. When I wake up with the sunrise, and go on a walk, I step through empty drink cans and those red party cups that are used for beer pong. I then see clothes of all kinds scattered around the Jacuzzi, which is partly caused by the truth or dare game we played. There's bodies lying in all the other rooms, even on the stairs, and it's like a scene from a zombie apocalypse movie, just without the blood and guts.

Once everyone is awake, we hydrate and cure our hangovers at the diner, down the road. When we arrive back at camp, we continue to conduct ourselves professionally around the campers.

39

NEVER A DULL MOMENT

There's never a dull moment at this place in the closeness of nature that's full of fake names and strange traditions, a place where the counselors love mud as much as the campers do. That is, until it gets in the cabin. Then nobody loves mud.

There are also deplorable traits that many of the kids have, such as finding something that doesn't belong to them, and then claiming it as their own. For instance, in the storeroom of Bunkhouse G, we now have an American football, volleyball and two Ga-ga balls that the campers have found and reserved for themselves.

Another critical mannerism is based on the collection of American football cards. The kids are using them for trading; either by swapping their cards with cards from other kids or exchanging cards for other items of value. I only start noticing the football cards when I see Josh's collection, though soon after that I discover that Malcolm and other campers from different cabins are doing the trading. These collectors have come out of the woodwork recently. Maybe they were concerned about confiscation if they started the craze at the beginning of the summer.

Josh is the brainiac of Bunkhouse G, who always seems to solve all the Rubik's cubes. He's also one of the most sensible campers when it comes to clean-ups. But Josh's cleverness is especially apparent when he tells me that he's researched and memorized how much every card is worth. This is in order for him to trade off his cheap cards for the more valuable ones and avoid giving away his most expensive cards. I think to myself that he'll become a successful businessman one day. The trading of these football cards, though, has generated dodgy deals, which has caused arguments between cantankerous campers. This free-play activity is the new obsession for many campers.

Another obsession, which has transpired lately, is that campers are very keen on obtaining sunflower seeds. The trading of this product starts with the older campers first. It's been witnessed that sunflower seeds are exchanged for money, but what's the fascination? This puzzles me, as chewing up the seeds and spitting out the shells, appears to be their only pleasure with them. On top of that, the campers aren't supposed to have money in their possession. Money should only be in the hands of the campers when purchasing a soda, or for leisure spending, during an offsite trip. This becomes a serious issue at camp, and Vince has announced that he's putting a stop to these dealings. Whenever counselors discover any bags of sunflower seeds, we're ordered to dispose of them immediately.

On a separate note, when we're away from the bunkhouse, numerous songs are often heard across the sports facilities. They are heard through the speakers, which aid the positive spirit. Everyone seems to have a great interest for the British singers that are Sam Smith and Ed Sheeran. The "Let It Go" song from the Disney film, *Frozen*, is an immensely popular song, especially with the girls' side. The "Shut Up and Dance" song, by Walk the Moon, is another summer hit that resonates with everyone.

I would say that the most popular and overplayed song of the summer so far, though, is the "Watch Me (Whip Nae Nae)" song by American hip hop artist, Silentó. It's prevalent with all the kids this summer, especially the campers in the younger divisions, who go nuts every time it comes onto the speakers in the dining hall at mealtime. They stand on their benches above their dinner trays and mimic all the actions to the song. This includes putting their arm out, with a fist, like they're driving a car. It's an impossible task to get them sitting back down and finishing their food, at least while their favorite song continues.

Another catchy tune that has the same impact on the children is the "Uptown Funk" song by Bruno Mars. It's gotten to the point where all of boys' side has their very own synchronized dance routine, to revel in particular parts of the song. The dancing has been choreographed, by Bobby during line-ups, who usually wears a red baseball cap with a gray or navy blue staff t-shirt, along with khaki shorts. He has a walky-talky attached to the back pocket of the shorts, which he uses to contact the head counselors as and when necessary. His trademark, though, is the black armbands that he wears around his elbows. They make him stand out, while he carries himself with so much charisma.

There are also some controversial songs that have been played through the speakers, and that have raised a few eyebrows. Controversia songs, such as "Baby Got Back" by Sir Mix-a-Lot and "Whistle" by Flo Rida, have sexual innuendos. "Blurred Lines" by Robin Thicke and Pharrell Williams has also been heard and in the media it has been considered to be one of the most provocative songs of the decade. I'm not quite sure what the head counselors, who organized these playlists, were thinking when adding these in.

I've also been equally surprised to hear that Camp Ace Invaders has its very own anthem. This two-minute-long jingle, with a saxophone melody, has most of the campers singing along in the dining hall when it plays.

"Life is great at Camp Ace Invaders,
Ace Invaders give me a cheer (hey!),
Life is great at Camp Ace Invaders,
Wish we could stay here, all year,
Wish we could stay here, all year!"

The campers also tell many riddles and jokes, though I can only remember a few. One riddle is from Ollie.

"Say fork," Ollie commands.

After I say fork, he asks: "Say fork five times?"

After I say fork five times, he asks: "What do you eat a soup with?"

You're supposed to be deceived into saying fork out of the quickness of the riddle, with little time to think. Having already heard this before, I say *fork* to Ollie, to make him appear clever to have outwitted me.

"What, you don't eat a soup with a spoon?" laughs Ollie.

155

There's one joke I hear two girls telling at free-play:

Q: Why do bees have sticky hair?

A: Because they use honeycombs!

Then I hear a simple, though effective, joke from Malcolm:

Q: What do you call a boomerang that won't come back?

A: A stick.

I have also been telling the limited number of jokes that I know, which are just about worthy enough to feature in a Christmas cracker. Here's one of them:

Q: What is the tallest building in the world?

A: The library. It has the most stories!

In terms of activities, there's been a one-off event that occurred spontaneously, following an announcement from Vince and it ran through the fifth activity of the normal agenda on a Thursday afternoon. It required stamina from each bunkhouse group, to run the lap of the sports complex, and to surmount the assault course style activities on our route. We were high stepping through truck tires and crawling underneath cargo net and through the mucky water of a large manmade trench. We completed each station together, as one bunkhouse, with other bunkhouses doing the same thing around us. It required teamwork above anything else; as we cheered each other on to endure the rest of the challenge. Like Bobby says: "Teamwork makes the dream work."

On the last leg of this event, we ran along the path that leads us down toward the main entrance of camp. Along this path, we ran through colored powder, thrown from the buckets of the rascally head counselors. By the end of that color run we were barely recognizable. But the kids were happy to know that it was shower hour next, while we counselors wait our turn for a shower at the next available opportunity.

On another randomly different note of late is the discovery of a creepy mask, belonging to Stan. It resembles the face of an elderly man wearing a baseball cap. There have been several occasions in Bunkhouse G when a camper has put the mask over their face and crept up on others, tiptoeing in the dark, in an attempt to scare them. Most of the time, from what I've witnessed, the intimidator is successful, and those on the receiving end jump out of their skin and shriek in terror, once they catch the haunting sight of the "elderly man."

40

TIME FOR SHART JOKES

Bobby has promised to come into our bunkhouse at nighttir share shart jokes. Before he enters Bunkhouse G on this particular r Robert and I, who are both on-duty, tell the kids they can t deliberately frighten Bobby—as long as they've brushed their teeth put their pajamas on, and are ready for sleep after.

Once the kids are ready for bed, we get ourselves ready to Bobby. It reaches 9:00 p.m., which is the time that's been arrange Bobby's visit. At this point, most of us are squatting between the bc beds, and the rest of us slither behind the corner of the walls, either i storage room, by the cubbies or by the showers. Logan nominates hir to put on *that* creepy mask.

I then switch off the main lights, making anyone from the ou assume that its bedtime in Bunkhouse G. But Logan shines a flash toward his face. All that can be seen is the outline of an elderly n face in the middle of the room, while the rest of us are hiding. Bobby enters.

"Hello, guys…guys…where are you? Who's this?" asks a puz Bobby.

I expect paranoia crept in, as he walks closer to Logan. After one distressing minute for Bobby, I quickly flex my gangly arm to flick on the lights.

"AAHHH!!" roars Bunkhouse G, as we leap out to scare Bobby. He looks more dazed by the main lights brightening the room, than scared.

He then resumes the purpose of his visit, which is to share an accumulation of funny jokes about sharting that the kids evidently love. This year, the kids have graduated away from fart jokes, and have moved toward jokes that focus on gassy poop. And jokes that focus on the accidental follow-through on a wet fart. It can be a problem for someone with diarrhea and definitely problematic for an elderly person with incontinence issues. It's something that I never want to experience in reality.

The campers are delighted about being graduated up to shart jokes, with Bobby's approval. So begins the ritual that only Bobby and the kids are aware of. We all sit around in a circle on the floor, holding hands, and Bobby begins a sing-along that the kids learn to replicate:

"We're Bunkhouse G, and we use to fart, but now we've graduated, it's time to shart!" This ends in applause.

Bobby tells Malcolm to grab a roll of toilet paper, which Malcolm gladly agrees to. When he comes back with the toilet roll, Bobby takes it and places it in the middle of the circle.

Bobby then instructs the group to think about a shart joke. Everyone is in deep thought about this subject. Then when a joke is processed, we take some toilet paper. It can be as many squares of paper as we desire.

159

But having it in our hands gives us the opportunity to share our joke with the group.

Q: What's the definition of bravery? Ethan asks.

A: A man with diarrhoea, chancing a fart.

Q: Have you watched the movie, *Diarrhoea*? Malcolm asks.

A: It leaked, so they had to release it early.

This is just two of many jokes shared. One thing that hasn't been a joke to some campers, though, is catching the dreaded *pink eye*. The term is used for conjunctivitis. It's occurred occasionally this summer, in drips and drabs. A kid wakes up with red, blood-shot eyes, which can be itchy and sore. This isn't due to sleep deprivation. The unpopular *pink eye* is presumed by the campers as being caused by the passing of gas on their pillows. I let the kids believe in this myth. This can make the kids assume that it's the farts that have made a joke out of them.

However, the eye irritation is commonly an infection from dir particles, or from allergens, such as dust or pollen as the result of hand to-eye contact. In a couple of frightful situations, both eyelids were stuck together in the mornings, as if they'd been dabbed with wallpaper paste in the middle of the night by a malicious prankster. A course o chloramphenicol drops were swiftly commenced by the nurse. I Bunkhouse G, Jackson and Malcolm have been victims of pink eye. It' not the most dignified moment in a camper's life, as they spend a fe days in the camp's health center, in quarantine, until their contagious ey condition resolves. As for every camper, washing their hands regularly is another important message from this.

As we close in on the night, Bobby informs me and Robert on the porch that although these kids are some of the most hyperactive and frustrating campers to be around, they're also the funniest. Tonight's been a weirdly entertaining experience, which not only brings unity to the bunkhouse, but also awareness to me that this is actually one of Bobby's favorite bunkhouses.

41

THE CHANGE-UP

Due to the numerous firings over the summer, a shortage of staff has developed. This has caused colleagues from bunkhouses to be transferred temporarily to other cabins for ODs, while the summer camp does *emergency recruiting* by scouting capable counselors in the local areas to work in the final stages. Tigger informs me that I'm going to do an OD in Bunkhouse H for a few nights before the staffing numbers improve.

I take this opportunity as a good thing. Tigger chose me as a form of respect because he trusts me to be responsible for safeguarding the welfare of children from another cabin overnight, as well as my own campers from Bunkhouse G, in the daytime.

Being in Bunkhouse H becomes an interesting experience and one that's unique in its own way. I'm introduced to new games, directed by the campers. A popular card game that Bunkhouse H plays together in a circle is "Mafia." In this game, a camper is nominated as "the moderator," and they take a card from the deck to represent each other player. The cards should include a red king to represent a "detective" and a red queen represents a "doctor." The rest of the cards are black number cards, indicating the "mafia" and red number cards, indicating the "citizens." The moderator then passes a card out to each player, face down. The players then look at their cards but keep it a secret for the duration of the game. The game has two phases; "nighttime," when the mafia secretly *murder* a citizen and "daytime" when the citizens vote to eliminate a Mafiosi suspect.

The moderator then tells the group to lie on their beds, face-down with their eyes shut, for *nighttime*. Then the moderator tells the mafia to wake up. The mafia players then acknowledge each other and determine, with hand gestures, which citizen will be killed. The moderator then tells the mafia to sleep and for the detective to wake up. The detective then rises and points to the moderator who they suspect is in the mafia, and the moderator responds with a thumbs up or thumbs down. The moderator then tells the detective to sleep and the doctor to wake up. The doctor then points to a player or themselves, and the moderator confirms whether that is who the mafia voted to kill.

Next, the moderator tells the group to wake up and come back to the circle for *daytime*. When everyone is sitting in a circle, the moderator has to narrate short stories on the spot, involving members of the group, and reveals the player that has died in the night. During one game in Bunkhouse H, Tyler, the moderator, reveals the victim, using his own imagination.

"Kyle was at a restaurant and after taking a bite of his burger, he fell on the floor, choking on the patty. Luckily, Nick was on the table next to him and saved him from death…but when Nick left the restaurant, a lion that escaped from the zoo, came out of nowhere. It jumped on Nick and ate him!"

Whoever voted to kill me, I hate you!" says Nick, amidst the laughter.

Nick and those who die in this round are eliminated, unless they're the individual that the doctor voted to be saved from death. A citizen then has the chance to accuse a player of being a member of the mafia. The accuser must then be seconded by another citizen and if this happens, the accused player is allowed to plead their case. After that, all players vote for the accuser to die, or the citizen, and the majority rules. The kid receiving the most votes then has to reveal their card to the group. The detective can then use this information to accuse members of the mafia, but they cannot be too obvious, or the mafia will kill them next. The game continues in the same way, with players returning to their beds and taking votes when they're entitled to. The citizens win if they manage to kill all the mafia and the mafia win if they manage to kill all the citizens.

At first, I think the game is quite inappropriate for a group of 10- to 11-year-olds to play, considering that the mafia is renowned for being ruthless and sinister criminals. The campers shouldn't be referring to themselves as such people. But I spectate and let the game continue. Just like shart jokes, I feel that this game is part of the DNA of Camp Ace Invaders, forever to be passed down from older campers.

A protocol that's used in cabins, including Bunkhouse H, is the TFK box. Bobby explains that the TFK box is given to a dysfunctional bunkhouse, and in the box, the campers and counselors can put both positive and negative messages on paper about something they've seen or how someone has acted in the cabin. It's been enforced in some of th bunkhouses where campers have been difficult to supervise and have stressed out their counselors. Bobby explains in a secretive lecture to the male counselors that TFK is an abbreviation for "The Fuck Kid." This is the phrase that possibly every counselor has felt like saying to a kid at some point this summer, though this abbreviation needs to have a meaning of less rudeness if it's questioned by the campers. It's suggested that this abbreviation should be referred to as something like "Treats for Kids," since they'll be rewarded for improving their behavior. If no negative messages are in the box, for a single day, then that day is added to the streak of good behavior within the bunkhouse. When a bunkhouse reaches their target number of days of 100 percent positivity, they earn themselves a party.

It's an initiative that's apparently had satisfying outcomes for counselors within the cabins, and its sole purpose is to get all members of the bunkhouse cooperating with each other better. My bunkhouse has never been given the TFK box, but *we counselors* have threatened the group with the possibility of bringing in the TFK box, when there have been moments of unacceptable behavior. The kids don't want this enforcement to happen, as it's something that doesn't bode very well with the parents if they find out.

Something else that's been used specifically in Bunkhouse H is the "last words." In turns, a camper talks about each of their fellow campers and predicts what they'll end up doing with their lives in the future. On the times I see this happen, when everyone is tucked under their duvets, campers are labeled with intelligent, high-earning professions, such as an investment banker and a manager of a business. Noah and Tommy are considered to become professional baseball players, since they excel in the softball and wiffle ball competitions. Two boys say that Shawn will end up being a professional dancer. They say this because they know Shawn hates being referred to as a dancer.

Shawn is a sensitive kid who gets easily upset, and because of this, he's often teased by the others. I find myself diffusing a couple of situations when I've witnessed the mocking. I see Shawn with teary eyes, moaning into his pillow.

Then, on my last OD night at Bunkhouse H, I hear Tyler say very sensible and caring words.

"Everyone should be enjoying this summer together, and we only have 10 days left to make this a great summer for all of us. No one should be picked on and singled out, especially Shawn, with the dancer thing said to him. And even though Shawn has refused to say his last words for the day because he's upset, my last words are for Shawn."

I thought this was a very touching and admirable thing for Tyler to say, and it was a great way to end the night. Shawn is a camper whom I'll be looking out for. I want to make sure he's enjoying himself for the rest of the summer.

42

THE COLOR WAR

"What the hell was that?" I say in confusion as I sit up in bed.

I jump off the bunk and look at my phone. It's 6:30 a.m.

There's chanting, with high-pitch whoops, which is constant and coming from outside. The sound of drums and tambourines accompany it. It's heard on the speakers and gets everyone awake in no time.

All of Bunkhouse G then walks over to where the excitement is taking place, with most of us still in our pajamas. We notice that all the other bunkhouses are doing the same.

The roaring, screeching and drumbeats are getting louder, the closer we get. It finally becomes apparent that it's coming from what looks like two teepees, located just in front of Maple Lagoon. A group of head counselors, dressed up in dance regalia and headdresses, to represent a Native American tribe, are parading out in front of the two teepees and creating the stereotypical Indian war cry. Everyone who's woken up is now surrounding the head counselors in their costumes.

Moments later, we all hear the trotting of a horse. It seems to be coming from the entrance of the campground.

Suddenly two tall, white, powerful stallions trot their way over to the waterfront, pulling a carriage full of other head counselors, who are dressed as cowboys. They're equipped with toy guns and are pretending to fire their weapons as they ride past.

"Yeeee-Hawwww! Yeeee-Haa! Yeeeeeeee!"

Soon, Vince and Marie come out in their usual sports attire, between the group of Native Americans on the left and the group of cowboys on the right.

"Good morning, everyone...and welcome to the 2015 outbreak of Color War!" shouts Vince.

The announcement is met with screams from every kid and counselor. Campers everywhere are babbling in a foolish and excitable manner. Color war is considered to be the pinnacle moment of the summer camp experience. It involves a whole week of activities, contested between two teams. Other years it's been red Pixar versus gold DreamWorks, red DC versus gold Marvel and red Jedi Knights versus gold Avengers. This year, the theme derives from a historical conflict (featured in western movies), between the cowboys, wearing red, versus the Indians, wearing anything yellow, to represent gold. This whole week will involve competitions, associated with the activities that normally take place on the camp's sporty complex.

Vince and Marie announce who the captains and lieutenants will be for each team. They've been decided by the head counselors, based on who has been the most impressive counselors and considered to be the most suitable for the role, in terms of leadership. Each team will have a total of three captains and three lieutenants, who'll boost their team's morale with motivational speeches. The captains will also decide which campers will participate in each competition for their teams. Each campe must be assigned to at least five competitive events during Color War. This is easily feasible, since there will be many team-sport events happening.

It would be fantastic to have the recognition of being selected as a captain or lieutenant, even though it'll increase the pressures within my job role. But as it turns out, I'm not picked. Beefy and Erica, however, are two captains for the Indians, and Nate is a captain for the Cowboys, along with Gavin, who's a lieutenant. I'm informed, by Tigger, that I'm a Red Cowboy, along with half of Bunkhouse G, and I'm provided with four red t-shirts in my size with a well-illustrated Color War logo on the front, displaying a western cowboy hat and an Indian headdress.

Over the next week, there's an upsurge in the positive spirt of the camp. The events are fiercely contested, but most importantly, the campers have a blast. The Red Cowboys are decked out in red from head to toe, while the Gold Indians shimmer in their yellow outfits. All campers have face paint, wigs, and other accessories of both colors that they obviously brought with them this summer in anticipation of this annual spectacle.

In the waterfront and poolside area, there are individual races and kickboard relays. In one event, a swimmer falls behind a bit, but her team is still there encouraging her to finish strong and give it her all. That girl in the Mohican division loses the race, but pops out of the pool with a grin so big that it brought smiles to everyone who watches. This is a great example of what happens here during Color War. Your team gets behind you and pushes you to the finish line.

A track is lined out on the lacrosse field that hosts individual sprints and relay races. Everyone gives 100 percent and runs their hearts out, including me during a "counselor relay race," which the Red Cowboys win, to my joy.

I also find myself refereeing a Middy boys' soccer game. The game finishes 2-1 to the Indians, and it's fun to be involved in a sports event that's close to my heart. Plus, there's no foul-mouthing to the ref, which I'm gladdened by.

Dustin is undoubtedly the least sporty camper in my bunkhouse, and arguably, the division. This isn't due to his chunky build. It's more his lack of interest in sports. He very rarely takes part in ball games in his free time, and instead, does a lot of things by himself, such as arts and crafts activities. But even Dustin shows moments of brilliance during the Color War. This happened in a Middy wiffle ball match. In this specific match, Dustin manages to help the Red Cowboys gain a ton of points.

He hits a triple, and the ball goes over the wall of the mini-stadium, which only a handful of campers of his age group have been able to achieve. In the "fielder" position, he also stops the ball with his feet twice before catching the last two batters out to win the match, against all odds. Dustin is a hero on this particular day and is greeted by hugs from all his teammates after the match, which is incredible to see. It's also nice for Dustin to prove to the other campers that he's not that hopeless kid when it comes to sport.

And how could I forget about the Ace-athon? This is the camp's mega relay race. This fun-filled competition has every single player representing their respective teams. There are 56 events scattered across the sports complex for this relay. Among the 56 objectives for both teams, a team needed to successfully complete a section of the high ropes course, and then a camper needed to hit a bullseye in archery, while another team of campers dive to the bottom of the swimming pool to pick up eight spoons. Each challenge ignites a shot of adrenaline to the heart of the competitors. Once the players complete an obstacle for their team, they're required to sprint over to the next station with their baton, and place it into the hand of the next player/s to start their task. Whether you were building a tower out of 50 Lego bricks or running around the a Ga-ga pit with an entire roll of toilet paper wrapped around you, every single player mattered in this three-hour competition and every single event affects the accomplishment of this race. Even though I was lingering around the waterfront for much of it, the race went down to the wire the whole way and there was lead changes happening at every turn, which were acknowledged by cheers from each team taking the lead. But in the last few challenges, the Gold Indians were ahead and crossed the finish line, beating the Red Cowboys by a mere one minute and 50 seconds.

Throughout the week, in the art department, counselors are making creative banners and plaques to represent their teams. I've contributed my creativity to the Red Cowboys' banner, by adding to the colorful background, featuring a crystal blue sky, above a golden desert, with mountains in the distance, and in between, cacti are standing like silent sentinels with tumbleweed rolling by. This landscape is the background to a cowboy swinging his lasso in the air, while riding a rearing horse. The work looks more and more eye-catching by the day and everyone's eager to see the presentations of the spectacular artwork in the penultimate event of Color War.

Everyone has feelings of inspiration at camp over the five days. To see groups of kids rally around one another in the true spirit of competition and do it in a way that's uplifting and encouraging, is awe-inspiring. It's made me realize how our goals in life require teamwork. It's not just about us. We need to avoid selfishness. We need to stay connected with people, and this shouldn't just be via technology but in the purest form. It's the way it should be, and it exists at Camp Ace Invaders.

43

THE COLOR WAR FINALE

The race between both teams in this year's Color War is close, based on the daily announcements of point tallies. It'll be decided at the singing competition on the final night. Before the singing event, though, is the last meal of the Color War. We're informed that this is to be a "silent meal." Neither team is allowed to speak a single word and will be penalized points if they utter a sound. There's no music, no chatter, no laughter. Counselors do their best to calm the excitement in the dining hall from the sniggering campers.

"Shhhhhh."

Despite having hundreds of people in the dining hall, it's oddly noiseless at a place where the campers are usually dancing and singing on their tables to the music surrounding the hall. Many campers cleverly bring paper and pens to write their conversations down. I can sense that the campers are desperate to talk, but they know that every word spoken will lose their team points. Seeing the desperation in the faces of the campers makes it a hilarious sound of silence.

Later in the evening, both teams enter the sports hall, dressed in their cowboy and Indian colors for the finale. There's a sense of elation, and true Color War pride. This is it. Everyone knows it.

First of all, the art teams present their plaques and banners. They're truly works of art. A worthy round of applause follows after each of their unveilings. Then it's time for the singing competition, and for both teams to put into practice what they've learned throughout the Color War. Memorizing and singing the lyrics to these songs have required a lot of dedication, discipline, and patience from everyone.

The counselors, especially the captains and lieutenants, have relentlessly encouraged and motivated those who were noncompliant. This is so that the team can all collaborate *as one* in the daily singing practices throughout Color War. Now, we're about to put so much meaning into every verse. Half the hall is a field of gold, and the other half is a sea of red.

In an alternating process, both teams sing the songs that they've been rehearsing in free periods during the week. The songs have been created and taught by the CIT girls and boys and they are sung without any instrumentals. The first song from the Red Cowboys goes like this:

Verse 1 Got a wakeup call from the enemy,
So, we rode up on our stampede,
The camp was split into two teams,
Red Cowboys won't face defeat.
Chorus Gold Indians you don't stand a chance,
Stop doing your rain dance,
Your teepees will fall,
Everybody knows our music's better,
You can't get help from nature,
Red Cowboys can't be stopped.

Verse 2 Navajo, Mohican, Cherokee,

All your tribes will face defeat,

You always lose at your own games,

It's time to go back to the Great Plains.

Chorus

After the first Gold Indians song, it's the second song from the Red Cowboys. It's sung to the beat of "That's My Kind of Night," by Luke Bryan, and it goes like this:

Verse 1 Welcome to the wild, Wild West. Saddle up,

Join us for our ride on the way to the top,

Watch out for our stampedes and our tumbleweeds,

The Cowboys are wanted dead or alive,

Guns and rifles will conquer your tribes,

We'll leave you in the dust, so hats off to us,

Yee-Haa!

Chorus Howdy Y'all the Red Cowboys—

Are here to take the victory,

We'll win this war because we've got Woody and Jesse,

So, come on over if you wanna see a rodeo,

Our lassos swinging in the air,

We've got good aim so beware,

Come after us if you dare,

Cowboys cannot lose this fight; red team will win tonight.

Verse 2 The sheriffs will lock you up downtown,

Watch out for Billy the Kid—he's all around,

Say goodbye to your land,

'Cause we are in command.

Chorus

The Gold Indians sing their second song after this. Then the Red Cowboys sing their final song. This song is known as the "Alma Mater," and it involves beautiful lyrics that embody the feelings that we all have as our summer is coming to an end:

Verse 1 As the days are fading, and we try to move on,
Hoping to find a star that we can wish upon,
Cause in those winter nights when I'm all alone,
I'll be thinking of the place that I can call my home.
Bridge But in the next few days we'll go our separate ways,
Tears fall from our eyes as we start to say goodbye.
Chorus Summer '15,
Our journey's ending but there's always you and me,
As days wind down and colors fade out,
How do I survive without you now?
Camp Ace Invaders Color War,
A summer that I'll have forever more,
An unexplainable,
Soon to be,
Memory.
Verse 2 As we stand here, looking at the faces around,
At this amazing place, and friendships we've found
I have been changed because of you,
Even when I didn't know I needed you.
Bridge
Chorus

The Gold Indians then poetically convey themselves in their Alma Mater. The lyrics included:

Chorus Ace Invaders are far from ordinary,
Nothing can compare,
Cause this isn't the end of our story,
I'll leave a page for you so don't worry.
I'm telling you to take one look at what we've been through,
Just you keep in mind,
That a piece of you will always remain here,
Cause going on without you will always be my fear.

Both songs are sung brilliantly, in the team's collaboration. They were pitch-perfect. The songs also left campers emotional with tears rolling down their faces. This is because they know their summer is drawing to an end. They are consoled by their counselors.

Then there's a tense few moments for both teams in the sports hall. We stay seated on the floor, waiting patiently for the results, while watching a row of head counselors doing the judging in their chairs on the stage. The judges have to discuss the final verdict. Which team is going to claim victory in the Color War?

And then the results came in. First, Vince announces that the Gold Indians have prevailed in winning their team the greater share of points for the artwork. But now Vince announces the final total of points that have been tallied throughout the week.

"On 4124 points is the Red Cowboys. On... 4103 points...is the Gold Indians. Red Cowboys have won Color War 2015!"

Frantic cheers in the sea of red instantly follow, with many shoulder rides for the campers in celebration. "We Are the Champions," by Queen is the song on the speakers that welcomes our celebrations. The feeling we're experiencing are another part of the story that we're writing together.

What amazes me in the sports hall on this night is to see the empathy of the red team embracing their friends on the gold team. This a moment beyond the competition that shows true friendship and respect. I see honor and goodwill, pride and compassion. Kindness matters more than winning and having the *bragging rights*. An authentic friendship is more important than competition. This is the essence of Camp Ace Invaders.

Tears are shed by campers on the red team for winning this five-day battle, and some tears are shed over the gold team's loss and the heartache of defeat. But the main reason why the campers are teary-eyed is because they all know that the end of Color War signifies the end of summer 2015. And for counselors and those in their last year as campers it could be their last ever summer here. What we've all gone through will be with us forever, but for now, it's about merging the two teams together into one wonderfully unified camp for the last four days.

44

THE AWARDS

Despite a lot of frustration during the supervision of the campers, I'll never forget the motivational words that head counselor, Randy, says to Robert, Nate, Brett, and me before he leaves Camp Ace Invaders. Randy had to leave camp a couple of weeks early, to return to his full-time job in Mexico. Before he leaves the camp, though, Randy makes sure he pays Bunkhouse G a visit.

"These boys are having the most fun, and you four are all hidden gems."

When Randy says these words to the four of us, it definitely creates a satisfied feeling within me, and makes me feel like all the hard work has been worthwhile. On numerous days this summer there's been an award for the counselor of the day, and whoever it's awarded to (whether they like it or not) wears the red-and-blue "Superman" cape with pride, which symbolizes this mini-accolade. There's also a tribute to the counselor of the week, every Friday evening line-up, which is when the group leaders of each division honor a particular colleague who has impressed them.

I never receive praise in these forms throughout my summer experience, and I start to realize that many of the counselors, who are commended, have a certain character about them. Their gregarious personalities gain them popularity because it's known to everyone.

On the other hand, there's me. I'm more of an introverted person. But I'm still a motivator, a teacher, and an enthusiast to the campers in the Middy division, as much as the next counselor. And having the pleasure of going on excursions with other counselors is evidence of my likable persona. I'm not crushed by disappointment when colleagues are praised for work that I feel I've contributed to. Instead, I continue to be a team player. I still feel proud of my contributions, and my efforts don't go completely unnoticed, which is evident by Randy's pleasing comment.

And then came the Ace Awards—an awards show dedicated to showing appreciation to the kids and counselors. This serves as a closing ceremony for the camp. Vince presents the awards in a black suit, alongside Marie in a shimmering purple dress. Everyone else in the audience dresses smart and the evening awards for the campers include "funniest comedian," "best hair (awarded to a Sideshow Bob lookalike in the Navajo division)" and "best siblings" of the year. There were also awards for "sports girl" and "sports boy" of the year and the biggest accolade, being the "camper of the year" (for each division). The show was just like a Hollywood-esque celebrity show. After the winners beat their campers in the nominations, they walk along the red carpet, down the middle of the sports hall, until they get to the stage where they meet Vince, Marie and the "paparazzi."

The accolades are then awarded out to the counselors. I'm delighted for Robert, who's one of the 20 individuals who receive the title of "counselor of the year" and are proudly presented with plaques. I'm pleased for Robert because, to me, he stood out as one of the most enthusiastic and passionate staff members. He did everything asked of him, by the book. He used nights off to spend extra time with the kids, and to help the counselors who were on-duty. And he engaged with the campers in such a heartwarming and pragmatic way.

45

SUMMER RECOLLECTIONS

The clock is counting down to the final day of summer at Camp Ace Invaders. I draw on some recollections that are fresh in my mind before I leave this place. And my head is full of pictures from the last eight weeks that I'll take away with me—pictures from this incredible sanctuary that'll make many more amazing memories for campers and counselors for years to come. First, I think about how fortunate I've been to be living with the other counselors in Bunkhouse G. The counselors I can now call my friends.

"You dingus!"

This is a common catchphrase expressed by Robert in his Yorkshire accent. Robert says this more so in frustration at campers, such as the times when they've not folded their clothing properly, or when they've ruined the cubbies by grabbing one item of clothing from the top shelf.

"Put wood in the hole."

This is another funny saying by Robert. It's an expression which can separate an English northerner away from the Yanks and an English southerner like me. This saying has the same meaning as *shut the door* since doors are typically made out of wood and fit into an opening that resembles a hole. Another English saying that's caught on at camp is *geezer.*

"Oi. Geezer!"

This is often said by Nate, in his Pennsylvanian accent, and it puts him into hysterics. To Nate, geezer means a cranky old man, which Americans interpret it as, but to guys of my age in England, geezer can be a friendly way to call your male pals.

As counselors, we have to be fun and funny, but also responsible and serious and we've enforced a level of firmness when we've needed to. We've set rules so that the kids mind them, yet we make time for foolishness and rule-bending. The counselors know when to be professional. And when it gets too late in the night for chit-chat, we have to put our stern faces on and give lectures to the misbehaving campers. Brett can be the most authoritative figure in the cabin, and on one particular OD night, the kids drive him crazy, which leads to a rant that any angry teacher would be proud of.

"This has got to stop! Sometimes, I feel like I'm talking to a brick wall! You need to listen to us more and set good examples at camp. You could become role models to the campers in the younger divisions. But instead, you decide to be so obnoxious! Okay, this doesn't go for all of you. Josh, Stan, and Ollie are generally well-behaved campers, and always work hard in the clean-ups. The rest of you are letting down the whole of Bunkhouse G. Especially you, Malcolm. I cannot, for the life of me, believe that you got a camper of the year award, last year. You've really gone downhill with your attitude this summer."

Brett says his rant in a louder voice than normal. He continues for another couple of minutes, with the bunkhouse dead silent and the campers reminded of the times when they aggravated him. But these episodes don't seem to affect the good rapport between the campers and

counselors. The kids adore our fun nature in the daytime, when the c
has its more lighthearted moments.

Regardless of all the mischievousness from the children
summer, there was one episode that I found comical. It was v
Jackson managed to get his hands on a poster of a female profess
wrestler, named Paige, which came out of a magazine. Paige is from
WWE and it's evident, from the poster, that she wears a limited am
of wrestling attire. Even at 11 years old, Jackson is adamant that he w
the poster displayed on the wall above his bed. I catch him on
occasion kissing the female's lips. It then got to the stage where sor
the campers offered their football cards in exchange for having the p
above their beds and *spending a night with Paige*. I let them continue
pursuits. Eventually, though, the poster vanishes out of the cabin, r
to be returned. I never found out what happened to Paige.

My mind then wanders back to the stunning features of M
Lagoon and the speedboat that I rode in with a boat speciali
remember the breeze blowing in my face and running through my ha
was awesome as I took in the view that's surrounding the campus.
name of the waterfront derives from the sugar maple foliage that e
the glistening water. The sap of the trees belonging to the foliage ca
the primary source for maple syrup—a popular condiment at cam
pancakes and waffles. At sunset, the water looks like a scatterir
diamonds as the light reflects onto it. It presents a beautiful appear
every night—picture perfect.

I then recollect on the many funny line-ups that I had the jo
watching, along with the rest of the boys' side. They are nearly al

led by Bobby. He's a great entertainer for us, and we all eagerly wait for him to weave his magic of humor each day.

"Keep your junk in your trunk!"

This is a catchphrase that Bobby says, in response to the reports from disgruntled counselors, about campers running out of the showers naked and doing the "helicopter." Bobby reenacts this awkward scene, but with clothes on, of course.

"Drink plenty of water! Keep hydrated! I need it. You need it to survive. This is how easy it is!"

Bobby lectures these words to us on a hot summer's day, and successfully attempts levity by downing a whole 500ml bottle of water within 30 seconds.

"Cover yourselves in sun lotion. Reapply every two hours. You don't want to be stumbling around looking like a red lobster from your sunstroke! This is how easy it is!"

Bobby expresses these words to us on another hot summer's day, while squirting out an entire bottle of sun lotion over his face, arms, and legs. These hilarious, overdramatic acts were memorable, and they've made everyone's summer. Bobby is interesting, funny, affirmative, informative, and engrossed in giving the campers the best possible summer experience.

He's even hosted his own show, "Late Night with Bobby," which has been by far the most anticipated evening show of the summer, with similarities of the famous American TV show, *Saturday Night Live*. It involves Bobby doing some stand-up comedy and featuring in a hilarious array of YouTube videos, which also presents charismatic head counselors and campers. There are skits that referenced everything funny about camp, which Bobby orchestrated prior to that night. These skits included a reenactment of dumb games that campers play, including "elimination." Obviously it's not just campers in bunkhouse G that get a thrill out of being human bowling pins. There was also footage of the invasion from the dinosaur "candy gods," which the kids now find the funny side to. Plus, another video revealed a trailer to a gripping horror movie, involving a group of members from Camp Ace Invaders that are stranded in the woods. There was plenty of suspense as the group was surviving from the close attacks of a zombie infected Vince. There was a terrifying perception of Vince in the trailer that is no different to how the campers must've felt when they were caught by him with sunflower seeds or caught getting out of song practice during Color War. It was still humorous to see the *normally* approachable Vince in this way.

Every camper and staff member was in hysterics throughout the show and even counselors who were off duty stayed to see it. Most of us name it as the best show of the summer. And this adds to the many compliments that I could give Bobby. I don't think anyone can imagine a summer here without him. He's not just an associate director. He's the life and soul of Camp Ace Invaders.

I also recall some other evening shows that I found entertaining. "Ace Invaders Have Talent" is a mimic of the television show, *Britain' Got Talent* or *America's Got Talent*, with two head counselors dressed in suits, portraying overly enthusiastic TV hosts. The stars of that night' show include a female counselor, called Joanna, singing pop star Adele' smash hit, "Rolling in the Deep." There was also a talented, synchronize dance act, performed by the CIT girls. This involved moves on the aeria hammocks attached to the ceiling and with impressive skills with simple props, such as hula hoops and umbrellas.

Another evening show that turns out to be an amusing spectacle is "Minute to Win It." A boy and girl represented each division and the crowd cheered on their campers that competed in a number of challenges for great prizes. Competitions included the buzz wire game and trying to get a cookie off their forehead and into their mouths without using their hands. Each contest was a minute long and it was a brave effort, especially from the Freshmen and Junior campers, to beat the clock with everyone watching and at times, laughing. After several rounds of head to heads, picked at random, the competition narrowed down to two campers—a CIT girl and a boy from the Collegiate division. For the last round, a hundred balloons were placed around the two campers and they had to pop as many balloons as they could with their butts. It was neck and neck with the clock ticking, but, in the end, the boy won on the judges' scorecards.

These memories help me to remember the importance of staying connected with people. This summer, I owe my happiness and enjoyment to every member of the summer camp, who's been positive and made me feel like a valued and important addition to their summer.

46

THE LAST GOODBYES

It's the morning of the final day at camp. All the duffle bags are ready for the kids on the porch. It was imperative to complete this and have the bags inspected by the head counselors yesterday, as the campers are leaving by noon today. They're going to leave in the same buses that dropped them off, all those weeks ago.

Looking back to a few years ago, I never would've thought that an American summer camp would pop up on my radar. And in mid-March this year, I still hadn't been placed at a summer camp, and I was starting to get worried that I would never get placed at a camp. That was until Camp Ace Invaders gave me *the call*. The call to adventure required me to cross the threshold, away from my ordinary world, and to this *special world*.

I had to be at camp by mid-June, but a lot had to be done before that. I was organizing my flights, getting my visa sorted, and leaving the country on my own. It's been the biggest step of my life. But throughout the long process of preparing to get there, no matter what trials and tribulations were thrown at me, I've felt like it was something that I was destined to experience.

Upon arrival at camp, I was completely out of my comfort zone. In my first couple of weeks at Camp Ace Invaders, I met over 200 people, and that was pretty scary. But after the first day, when I arrived at the camp in Beefy's taxi, I was nowhere near as nervous because everyone I met was so welcoming.

In these two months, I had the most amazing weeks of my life, and the kids I looked after were the most fascinating and entertaining kids I've ever met. They made the distance from home bearable, even though I've had to deal with their disobedience and help them with their homesickness. I watched the campers' self-confidence grow, and I know that they'll go back home feeling more self-assured, having gone through this whole experience by themselves. That's what makes Camp Ace Invaders special for the children.

As time passed, my confidence as a general counselor grew, too. It helped that I was in a working environment that could change unpredictably and a daily routine that could alter without warning. It required me to apply myself and use my initiative.

I have also been able to achieve the healthy balance of less time on mobile devices and spending more time with people face to face. This summer camp experience, with its busy schedule and lack of access to Wi-Fi, has forced me to stay unplugged for most days.

Having now worked at camp, I know that life at camp is a place where face paint is the norm, where lasting memories and unbreakable friendships are made, and where each camper and counselor gets to feel like a hero at some point during the summer. You won't have to explain anything to the people who've been to camp because they know that their summer camp experiences changed them for the better. It fills them with so much pride to be able to wear their summer camp shirts every single day, rain or shine.

The summer camp has enabled campers to sing along to what's played on the speakers, instead of closing out the world with headphones. They talk to each other face to face, rather than communicate through texts. And their connections with each other aren't limited by megabytes of data—it's by the length of their stay at camp. By unplugging the digital world, the campers gain confidence, have fun, and most importantly, form lifelong relationships in the real world.

I'm sure I speak for every camper when I say that Camp Ace Invaders has a special place in their hearts. It's like a getaway vacation for the campers where they have extra freedom. And the counselors are like the older brothers and sisters who support the campers through their experience, so that they never feel upset, secluded, or doubtful about anything.

When the kids I looked after for so long, turn around to say their final goodbyes, I just about murmur a goodbye back to them. My eyes well up, and I have a lump in my throat. Then tears come tumbling from my eyes, for the first time this summer. They feel like family members leaving me behind—and now I feel emptier. I don't know if I'll ever see their faces again, but they all have a place in my heart, and I'll never forget them.

As I look around at this emotional time, I realize that my colleagues are also devastated by the fact that the summer has now come to an end. This just goes to show how powerful the camp has been and how grateful we are to have experienced and shared the memories we've made.

There's something special about working at Camp Ace Invaders. As a first-year international counselor, I had no idea what to expect, but from the moment I set foot on the campground, I realized that I was in a magical place—that the experience was incomparable to anything I've done before.

I've learned a great lesson from this experience—that life's about taking chances, even if you have a high level of uncertainty about them. The decision I made to take on this experience now feels like a pivotal moment in my life. I knew I had to write a book about this amazing experience one day.

SNAPS AT CAMP

In Bunkhouse G

The cliff diving

A tetherball match during evening line-up

Being creative in the art department   The dining hall

Ga-ga ball   Maple Lagoon waterfront

Wiffle ball

4th of July celebrations   The campers depart

ACKNOWLEDGEMENTS

Much love and thanks to my family, for all their support over the years and for the encouragement to keep me going with the writing for this book.

To all my friends in England for all the good times we've shared, especially all the drunken nights out. You know who you are, otherwise I'll let you know over a drink!

To Tottenham Hotspur football club, for all the entertainment they've brought me over the years, apart from the heartache.

To George Verongos for his helpful advice in the editing stage of the book and to Matt Rott who helped particularly in getting the present and past tenses right to suit the timelines for this memoir.

To Wayne Purdin for his attention to detail in the final editing phase of my book. He understood my reader audience and his input was valuable and just what I needed before the publication.

To Ansh Deb for working in such a timely and professional manner to create the amazing book cover design.

To Kindle Direct Publishing for being a great service for me in allowing me to format and self-publish my work.

To those I met and enjoyed my travels with along the East Coast of America—visiting New York City, Philadelphia, Miami, Orlando, Atlanta, Nashville, Washington DC, Baltimore, and Ocean City (in that order) as I go. There was an abundance of amazing sights to behold, from the Statue of Liberty, to the Rocky Steps of the Liberty Bell, to the glamorous scene around South Beach, to Universal Studios, to the Tennessee bars that play live country music, to the Lincoln Memorial. They were all amazing to witness and there was plenty of fun to be had after my summer camp experience ended. I will not miss that 17-hour Megabus ride from Nashville to Washington DC, though!

And many thanks to the Wild Packs team and the summer camp family. Without them, the summer of 2015 wouldn't have been as memorable, and the writing of this book wouldn't have been possible.

Printed in Great Britain
by Amazon

71577087R00123